MEET ME IN THE MORNING

Deepening Your Devotion to God

Dr. Lance D. Watson

Lance Watson Ministries
Richmond, Virginia

Unless otherwise indicated, all Scripture quotations are taken from the New International Version of the Bible.

Scripture quotations marked NKJV are taken from the New King James Version. Copyright 1982 by Thomas Nelson, Inc. Used by permission. All Rights Reserved.

Scripture quotations marked MSG are taken from The Message. Copyright 1993, 1994, 1995, 1996, 2000, 2001, 2002. Used by permission of NavPress Publishing Group.

MEET ME IN THE MORNING:
DEEPENING YOUR DEVOTION TO GOD

ISBN - 13: 978-0-615-28078-3
ISBN - 10: 0615280781
© 2009 by Lance Watson Ministries
Saint Paul's Baptist Church
4247 Creighton Road
Richmond, Virginia 23223-7344
www.myspbc.org

Printed in the United States of America. All rights reserved under International Copyright Law. Contents and/or cover may not be reproduced in whole or in part in any form without the express written consent of the Publisher.

Table of Contents

How to Use This Booklet 5
Thoughts on the Journey 7
Commitment 9
    The Perfect Lifeguard 10
    Single-Minded Devotion 12
    Self-Investment 14
    God's Direction for Our Daily Decisions 16
    God's Gracious Hand 18
    Pulling Nails and Weeds 20
Faith 23
    The Power of Faith 24
    Better Than A Birthday 26
    O Yes, You Can! 28
    The Other Side of Faith 30
    Tasty Faith 32
    Leaning Your Weight 34
    Faith's Final Exam 36
Sacrifice 39
    Spiritual Sacrifices – Part One 40
    Spiritual Sacrifices – Part Two 42
    Generous Grace Giving 44
    Pass the Fries 46
    Heavenly Treasure 48
    Sow and Grow 50
    Worthless Worry 52
Purpose 55
    The Main Thing 56
    Can't Do It Alone 58
    Big Rocks 60
    The "E-Church" 62
    A Legacy of Purpose 64

    Giant Icebergs 66
    Give Me the Details 68

Service 71
    Your Calcutta 72
    An Excuse to Serve 74
    Out of the Backseat 76
    From Squirting to Soaking 78
    Saving Starfish 80
    Glitzy Gifts and People Pleased 82
    Basin Theology 84

Thanksgiving 87
    Thank You, Thank You, Thank You 88
    Too Good to Keep to Ourselves 90
    A Recipe for Giving Thanks 92
    Thankful Praise to Our Good God 94
    An Attitude of Gratitude 96
    Taking the Time To Say Thanks 98

Appendix A: Suggestions for Family Devotions 101

Appendix B: Forty Day New Testament Reading Plan 103

Appendix D: Six Key Memory Verses 105

Appendix C: Tips for Bible Memorization 107

Appendix D: Personal Notes / Prayer Journal On Faith 109

Appendix E: Personal Notes / Prayer Journal On Commitment 111

Appendix F: Personal Notes / Prayer Journal On Purpose 113

Appendix G: Personal Notes / Prayer Journal On Sacrifice 115

Appendix H: Personal Notes / Prayer Journal On Service 117

Appendix I: Personal Notes / Prayer Journal On Thanksgiving .. 119

How to Use This Book

I am convinced that this is going to be a time of incredible personal and corporate spiritual growth for you and yours. When we do things like intentionally pray, systematically read, thoughtfully meditate, carefully memorize, and sacrificially give, we inevitably grow! Each of us, however, needs to actively and cheerfully play our part for this tremendous growth potential to be realized in our lives and church.

The following forty devotions are part of that opportunity for greater spiritual maturity, because they help keep God and the truth of God right where they belong—at the center of our lives and at the center of this church. Although the text is brief, don't rush this daily date with the Lord. Spend time in prayer before and after. Look up the verses and context in your own Bible, along with correlating passages that may come to mind.

Listen expectantly to God's Word and be eager to let His Spirit guide you. Even if you've never had a journal or taken notes on your spiritual journey before, consider using the blank pages in the appendices to record your experience as it relates to each theme. Insights, questions, victories, struggles, requests, confessions, personal growth plans, and much more might find its way into your spiritual journal.

Each of the six title pages, as well as Appendix B, presents a simple reading plan that will take you on a daily tour of the entire New Testament (NT) during these forty days. This averages out to a stretching but manageable 6.5 chapters per day. In case that seems too daunting, realize that there are more words in the edition of the newspaper than in the entire NT.

MEET ME IN THE MORNING

Certainly, reading God's Word is far more worthwhile and profitable (2 Tim 3:15-17).

You'll also notice a key memory verse on each week's title page. I want to invite you to hide these six key verses in your heart (Ps 119:11), so that we may collectively be "standing firm in one spirit with one mind...being one in spirit and purpose" (Phil 1:27; 2:2). Appendix C offers some tips to help you succeed with the memorization, although experience will be your best teacher.

Finally, each devotional concludes with a short discussion session designed to aid our small groups and usually a suggested family activity to drive home the truth under consideration. With a little preparation and some creative customization, your family time can be fun and meaningful. Please read Appendix A for some tips to maximizing these family devotions. If you're not using this booklet with your family, a group, or a friend, you can still use the discussion question to spur prayerful reflection and action. By embracing these things, we'll not only grow...but we'll be blessed in the process (Jas 1:25)!

DEEPENING YOUR DEVOTION TO GOD

Thoughts on the Journey

Dear Spiritual Traveler,

In 2008 during our Lenten Celebration, the Holy Spirit planted in my heart a question with which I have grappled. The question was very simply, "What is transforming about these experiences?" I realized then that outside of the inviting our members to participate in the weekly worship celebrations during Lent, there had been nothing fundamentally mapped out to make these days a meaningful, significant and transformative time: thus this devotional guide.

This guide is designed especially for your use during the forty days of this year's Lenten season. The topic for each week focuses on six ways that I pray we will all be transformed by the grace of God. Accordingly, you'll have the opportunity in your quiet time to explore a week of devotions on commitment, faith, sacrifice, purpose, service, and thanksgiving. All of these themes are intricately interwoven into the very fabric of every strong, growing, vibrant believer, family and church.

I believe that if we are truly to connect with God, each other, and the world— we need to increasingly absorb these qualities and their attendant actions into our lives and activities. My heartfelt prayer is that this little booklet, and especially the eternal truth it exposes, will help us do just that—ultimately leading each of us to be "on the grow" together by the power of God. I want to lead that charge!

On the Grow with You,
Pastor Lance D. Watson

Commitment

Memory Verse:
"The eyes of the LORD search the whole earth in order to strengthen those whose hearts are fully committed to him."
2 Chronicles 16:9 (NLT)

Reading through the NT in 40 Days:

- Matthew 1-5 .... Day 1
- Matthew 6-11 .... Day 2
- Matthew 12-17 .... Day 3
- Matthew 18-23 .... Day 4
- Matthew 24-28 .... Day 5
- Mark 1-8 .... Day 6

Christ is not valued at all—if He is not valued above all.
– St. Augustine

Day 1 – Commitment

The Perfect Lifeguard

"The eyes of the LORD search the whole earth in order to strengthen those whose hearts are fully committed to him." –2 Chronicles 16:9 (NLT)

As I pondered this verse, my mind wandered back to the time when I was trying to be certified as a lifeguard through the Boy Scouts. After weeks of preparation and days of intensive training, each candidate sat beside an experienced lifeguard while hoards of children frolicked in the camp lake. Perched on that stand with my eyes wide open, I feverishly scanned the water in a "Z" pattern for potential hooligans to rebuke or victims to rescue. Sitting erectly, I whispered to myself, "This is the real thing…lives are depending on me!"

After a while, however, the baking of the Michigan summer sun and the boredom of simply sitting took its toll. I didn't even get to blow my new plastic whistle. Bummer. My eyelids fluttered once, then twice. If it weren't for a sharp nudge from my trainer, I would have surely dozed myself out of lifeguard certification.

Fortunately, God is the perfect Lifeguard! His eyes see everyone and everything, and His loving gaze is drawn particularly to those who have fully committed themselves to Him. He doesn't look at them to condemn or crush, but to refresh and restore. The committed Christian life, therefore, is never a solitary or self-empowered endeavor, because God is always looking to bolster us and bear our load (cf. Matt 11:28-30; 1 Pet 5:6-7).

Even though the implication of this verse is that complete commitment may mean we sometimes feel depleted, it also

DEEPENING YOUR DEVOTION TO GOD

assures us that the mighty Lord stands ready to replenish us every time. Unlike those vulnerable kids under the sleepy care of this novice lifeguard, we can rejoice that "he who watches over you will not slumber…the LORD will watch over your coming and going both now and forevermore" (see Psalm 121)!

For Discussion: What might a heart "fully committed" to God look like today (think of Christ in 2007)? Are your motions and motives such that you "catch God's eye?" What benefits arise from full commitment?

Family Activity: Since this Lenten Season offers a great opportunity to develop deeper commitment and experiences its benefits, jot down, sign, and post in your home the aspects you'll commit to (e.g., daily prayer and family devotions; reading through the New Testament; memorize the six verses; attend all services, a small group, and the two Encounter gatherings; financial commitment; and inviting friends to church).

Day 2 – Commitment

Single-Minded Devotion

"Elijah went before the people and said, 'How long will you waver between two opinions? If the LORD is God, follow him; but if Baal is God, follow him.' But the people said nothing." – 1 Kings 18:21 (NIV)

Commitment is not as elusive or difficult as some initially think. In fact, everyone is committed to many things in varying degrees. Scripture and experience, however, testify that total commitment to the true and living God can be more difficult. That's partly because commitment to Him is to be our top and guiding pledge, requiring single-minded devotion and total dedication (e.g., Rom 12:1-2).

As we approach 1 Kings 18, many Israelites had followed King Ahab and Jezebel into wholehearted idolatrous worship of Baal. They remained passive while a death warrant was issued and carried out on God's prophets. Now, Elijah's question pierces their apathy and forces them to face up to their loyalty lapse. Until then, they had been double-minded, not willing to choose between God and Baal. Most of us have made the ultimate choice of our Master. And yet even we still need to periodically reaffirm and realign our allegiance.

"Double-mindedness" speaks of one who tries to split his or her energies between the struggle and system of the culture and the role and rule of Christ. Jesus announces in Luke 11:23: "He who is not with me is against me." Others, like James, also urge us not to vacillate between two allegiances:
"You adulterous people, don't you know that friendship with

the world is hatred toward God? Anyone who chooses to be a friend of the world becomes an enemy of God" (4:4; cf. 1:5-9; 4:1-10; Ps 119:113).

Divided hearts only multiply our problems!

On the other hand, we're called to serve a single Master (e.g., Matt 6:24) while we firmly "fix our eyes on Jesus, the author and perfecter of our faith" (Heb 12:2; cf. Ps 141:8; Matt 6:22). Let's not be like "the people [who] said nothing" to Elijah's challenge. Instead, let us be like those after the miracle in 1 Kings 18 who "fell prostrate and cried, 'The LORD—he is God! The LORD—He is God!'" (v. 39). You'll be on the winning side *every* time (v. 40)!

For Discussion: Brainstorm a full list of the various things you're committed to. Do or could any of those things contribute to double-mindedness? How? Pick one as an example and discuss a step you can take this week to cultivate more single-minded devotion to God.

Day 3 – Commitment

Self-Investment

"If anyone desires to come after me, let him deny himself, and take up his cross daily, and follow me. For whoever wishes to save his life will lose it, but whoever loses it for my sake will save it." –Luke 9:23-24 (NKJ)

Alan Greenspan who formerly directed monetary policy in our country once used a phrase that I never forgot; it was "irrational exuberance." He used this phrase to describe the bull driven technology stocks on the late nineties. When we pair that phrase with the steady bombardment of phony offers to "strike it rich instantly," it is painfully obvious that there are very few guaranteed investments in life. Perhaps the only one we ever really have some control over is the investment of *ourselves*. In today's text, Jesus gives us a five-part "investment prospectus" worth heeding.

"If anyone desires to come after me" – The first step to a self-investment with eternal dividends is a definite decision. We will never accidentally stumble into committed discipleship. We must desire the presence of God in our lives enough to make a resolute decision to follow Him wherever He leads, no matter the cost. Have you done that?

"Let him deny himself" – For your decision to "stick," you must fuel it with daring discipline. This means putting Christ above every other thing, idea, and person—even yourself. Are you doing that?

"…And take up his cross daily" – Self-denial is easy for a sprint, but more challenging for a marathon. That's why so many diets

DEEPENING YOUR DEVOTION TO GOD

fail! What we need is daily devotion. When it comes to Christian commitment, it's never better to "burn out than fade away." Are you?

"...and follow me" – Just as whimsical investments rarely produce, so your self-investment must center on a determined direction; namely, whenever and wherever the Lord leads you. Are you *really* following?

"...whoever loses [his life] for my sake will save it"—Do the previous four steps sound too daunting? Then consider this delightful dividend! Jesus offers an eternally abundant life when we consistently make a wise investment of ourselves (e.g., John 10:10, 28)! Are you?

For Discussion: Take a few quiet moments to meditate upon each part of Christ's challenge and the corresponding points and questions. As you're comfortable, share some successes and areas in need of growth.

Family Activity: Though nobody can fulfill this challenge for you, everyone benefits when commitment is a family affair. Read Josh 24:1-27. As you recite v.15 together, drive a stake in your yard and leave it there for the rest of this season as a tangible reminder of your self-investment.

Day 4 – Commitment

God's Direction for Our Daily Decisions

"Trust in the LORD with all your heart and lean not on your own understanding. In all your ways acknowledge Him, and He shall direct your paths." –Proverbs 3:5-6 (NKJ)

No matter your age or position, your life is teeming with decisions. This passage prescribes three commitments that prepare us to navigate the sea of questions we face each day. Taken together, obeying these commands yields a life that fully depends upon God and, therefore, fully enjoys His direction for our daily decisions.

"Trust in the LORD with all your heart"—First, we must accept God's dependability. If we don't *completely* rely upon the Lord with the totality of our being, we shouldn't expect His guidance. Halfhearted trust isn't trust at all, especially when it comes to trusting God.

"…do not lean [depend] on your own understanding"—As we accept that He is totally trustworthy, we should simultaneously admit God's wisdom into our lives. God *wants* to offer generous doses of wisdom when we ask in faith as a demonstration of our dependence on Him (Jas 1:5-8). Conversely, exclusive reliance upon our own intellectual resources blinds us to the direction of the only true Know-It-All!

"In all your ways acknowledge Him"—Because life is so complex and interrelated, we must acknowledge God's presence in *every* area to discern His leading in *any* area. Otherwise, how will we see His guiding hand? And why should we expect God to guide us at the crossroads of life if we ignore His leadership the rest of the time? Look for Him in all you do.

"...and He shall direct your paths"—As a result of sincerely practicing these principles, we can anticipate God's direction. What great news! Our Shepherd *will* guide us in the decisions of life as we consistently accept His dependability, admit His wisdom, and acknowledge (put first) His person and presence in our lives.

To Discuss and Do: Have each person finish the statement, "The decision I'm facing right now that I would most like to have God's direction in is..." Record the answers in your journal (Appendix E and discuss how you can apply these verses to experience God's guidance in those areas. Review the answers at the end of the 40 Days, which is Thanksgiving week. As we live lives of commitment between now and then, we'll be amazed at the gift of God's direction for our decisions. There will be even more things to be grateful for this year!

MEET ME IN THE MORNING

Day 5 - Commitment

God's Gracious Hand

"...the good hand of his God was upon him. For Ezra had set his heart to study the law of the LORD and to practice it, and to teach His statutes and ordinances in Israel." –Ezra 7:9b-10 (NAS)

Several times in the book of Ezra we read that God's gracious hand was firmly upon Ezra. God's hand is credited with blessing, strengthening, protecting, and guiding him (7:6, 9, 25, 28; 8:18, 22, 31). Today's verse reveals precious insight into why this preeminent scribe and priest enjoyed such tremendous provision and success.

"For Ezra had set his heart"—To begin, Ezra's whole life and ministry revolved around a resolute commitment to the Word of God. He did not treat Scripture lightly, but esteemed it enough to focus His full energies upon it. The three objects of this commitment follow.

"...to study the law of the LORD"—Zeal must be grounded in truth (cf. Rom 10:2). Ezra's certainly was. He focused his resolute commitment on real comprehension of the Word. Ezra's mastery of the meaning and implications of Scripture required diligent effort that was energized by his compulsion to know God and His will as revealed in His Word.

"...and to practice it"—Knowledge alone is inadequate. People merely "deceive themselves" when they know God's Word but don't allow it to change them (Jas 1:22). Ezra, however, demonstrated radical conformity to the Word (cf. Rom 12:1-2).

DEEPENING YOUR DEVOTION TO GOD

And like him, the one who learns *and* lives truth "will be blessed in what he does" (Jas 1:25).

"…and to teach His statutes and ordinances in Israel"—those who know and grow in the Word can't stop there. Instead, like Ezra (see Neh 8), they also need to commit to relational communication of the Word to others (e.g., Deut 6:4-9; Matt 28:19-20; Eph 4:15; Col 3:16; 2 Tim 2:2; Heb 5:12). Don't be content with just your own growth. Pass it on, so that "*we all reach unity in the faith and in the knowledge of the Son of God and become mature…*" (Eph 4:13).

As we live out a commitment to hear, heed, and herald God's Word, we can expect His powerful hand to bless us in His marvelous way and timing (cf. Matt 27:24-27; Rev 1:3)!

For Discussion: Which of Ezra's three commitments do you most need to "set your heart" toward right now? What practical steps can people take to advance in living out each of the three areas? What opportunities are available at Saint Paul's Baptist Church to help?

Day 6 – Commitment

Pulling Nails and Weeds

"Because we have these promises, dear friends, let us cleanse ourselves from everything that can defile [contaminate; pollute] our body or spirit. And let us work toward complete purity because we fear [soberly and humbly revere] God." –2 Corinthians 7:1 (NLT)

A pastor in the dreadfully poor country of Haiti illustrated the need for total commitment to purity by telling about a man who wanted to sell his house for $2,000. Another man wanted very much to buy it, but he did not want to pay the full price. After much bargaining, the owner agreed to sell the house for less than the original price with just one stipulation: he would retain total ownership of one small nail protruding from just over the door.

After several years, the original owner demanded the house back, but the new owner refused to sell. So the first owner went out, found the fresh carcass of a dead pig, and hung it from the single nail he still owned. For obvious reasons, the house quickly became unlivable, and the family was forced to sell the house back to the owner of the nail.

This parable graphically captures the need for "comprehensive Christlikeness." Whenever we knowingly agree to leave even one small nail of evil in our lives, we're bound to find rotting garbage on our front doorstep! Since "anyone…who knows the good he ought to do and doesn't do it, sins" (Jas 4:17) and "everything that does not come from faith is sin" (Rom 14:23), let's draw on God's power to yank out even the hidden nails! Then, rather than offending people with the "smell of death," we can be "a life-giving perfume" wherever we go (2 Cor 2:16)!

DEEPENING YOUR DEVOTION TO GOD

For Discussion: The "these promises" in 2 Corinthians 7:1 refer back to the aspects of the New Covenant mentioned in 6:14-18. Read those verses and discuss how they, along with the concluding phrase of 7:1, do or should impact your progressive growth of holiness (sanctification).

Family Activity: Instead of pulling nails from your house, go out and pull weeds from your yard. Talk about the process of "spiritual weeding" while you symbolically rid yourself of unwanted weeds (sins). Why do you pull them by the roots? What happens if you leave them? How do you prevent them?

"Give me 100 men who hate nothing but sin and love God with all their hearts and I will shake the world for Christ!" –John Wesley

Faith

Memory Verse:
"Now faith is being sure of what we hope for and certain of what we do not see." – Hebrews 11:1 (NIV)

Reading through the NT in 40 Days

- Mark 9-16 .... Day 7
- Luke 1-6 .... Day 8
- Luke 7-12 .... Day 9
- Luke 13-18 .... Day 10
- Luke 19-24 .... Day 11
- John 1-5 .... Day 12
- John 6-10 .... Day 13

FAITH is:

Forsaking All I Trust Him!

Day 7 – Faith

The Power of Faith

"This is the victory that has overcome the world—our faith."
–1 John 5:4 (NKJ)

We can become so preoccupied with the hazards, handicaps, and hindrances in the race of faith that we try to take detours or linger too long at rest stops along the way. But the collective testimony of the heroes in Hebrews 11 should encourage us: "Since we are surrounded by such a great cloud of witnesses [i.e., those in chap. 11], let us throw off everything that hinders and the sin that so easily entangles, and let us run with perseverance the race marked out for us" (Heb 12:1). The witness of those who have come before us spur us to endure in a life of faith in many ways, including by teaching us valuable lessons about living faith in God.

Faith Cleanses All Kinds of Pollution – Everyone in chapter 11 was dysfunctional like you and me. Rahab was a prostitute. Noah got drunk. Abraham and Isaac lied. Sarah laughed at God and then denied it. Moses murdered. David committed adultery. We could go on. But notice: nothing of their failures is mentioned in chapter 11! Can we collectively shout right there? When we trust Christ as our Savior, God cleanses our sin and gives us a new beginning (1 Cor 6:11). As a new creation, we have new power to accomplish new victories (2 Cor 5:17).

The pollution of our past is no handicap!

Faith Changes All Kinds of People—Hebrews 11 teems with

variety. Faith is found in men and women, the young and old, kings and commoners, the poor and wealthy, the highborn and illegitimate. "God does not show favoritism but accepts men from every nation who [by faith] fear him and do what is right" (Acts 10:34; cf. Rom 2:11; Eph 6:9). These faith heroes were different but united in daring to trust God, and in doing so, being forever changed by Him.

Faith Conquers All Kinds of Problems—The life of faith certainly has its challenges, but it also has great resources to bolster it. Faith enabled Enoch to stay pure in a defiled world, Noah to withstand national ridicule, Moses to fight government opposition, and Daniel to face a den full of lions. Although God doesn't work the same in every life, when He allows us to conquer problems, faith is always involved (Eph 6:16; 1 John 5:4).

Faith Conducts All Kinds of Potential—Faith does not create reality, but it is a conduit for God to work *His* reality into our lives. Faith released the potential for a shepherd boy like David to become a mighty king. Looking through spectacles of faith, we can see and seize all kinds of potential for ourselves and others to God's glory (cf. Matt 9:24).

For Discussion: How do today's four points help you obey Heb 12:1?

MEET ME IN THE MORNING

Day 8 - Faith

Better Than A Birthday

"Now faith is being sure of what we hope for and certain of what we do not see." –Hebrews 11:1 (NIV)

Do you remember how you felt, especially as a young child, when your birthday was approaching? If you were at all like me and my brothers growing up (we would talk about our birthdays all year!), you were full of excitement and anticipation. Why? Probably because you were confident that you would receive gifts, special visitors, and other delightful treats. Your parents had proven to be trustworthy in coming through for past birthdays, and you were certain they'd do so again.

There is some parallel to faith. Although Heb 11:1 is not a formal or exhaustive definition, it indicates that a significant feature of biblical faith is eager certainty about the unseen. Faith extends beyond what we learn from our normal senses to realities that have no material evidence but are real nonetheless (cf. 2 Cor 5:7). It gives us a genuine conviction about the reality of God's promises and a calm confidence that we will encounter them—the best gifts of all!

This faith, then, is not a complacent emotion or static energy but something lively and active. It impels us to reach out and lay hold of the spiritual realities that are *already* ours in Christ and to savor *now* the blessings awaiting us in the future. And because that kind of faith relies on God and *knows* He will "come through," it pleases Him (Heb 10:35-39; 11:6).

DEEPENING YOUR DEVOTION TO GOD

In the remainder of Hebrews 11 we're challenged to live lives of faith according to the pattern of people who demonstrated a firm confidence in God's promises even though they had not yet received the fulfillment of those promises (vv. 13, 26, 39). Faith presses us steadfastly on toward what God has for us now and in the future, no matter what we're currently feeling or facing (10:32-39; 11:27, 35-40; 12:2).

We've already received so many "unseen gifts" from God, and something far better than a birthday is coming. So let's get excited with "childlike faith" before a birthday (cf. Matt 11:25; 18:3; 19:14)!

For Discussion: Talk about how anticipating a birthday is and isn't like faith. Brainstorm promises and spiritual realities we have from God. Pick one that encourages you and think of it in the context of Heb 11:1.

Family Activity: Read Hebrews 11. Wrap up something special and leave it out until the end of this season as a reminder to exercise biblical faith.

Day 9 – Faith

O Yes, You Can!

"…you have never been this way before." –Joshua 3:4b (NIV)

A driver inched her jeep along one of the most treacherous roads in the Rocky Mountains. Approaching an extremely narrow pass with no guardrail, she contemplated turning around. "Nothing will keep me from plunging thousands of feet into that gorge," she quivered. Just then, she noticed a small sign posted on the ledge: "O yes, you can! Thousands have." Her jeep crept forward once again.

How many times have we balked along the path of faith because of fear?

Stronger faith is the antidote to strangling fear (cf. Matt 6:25-33). The lush valley is often just on the other side of the treacherous cliff. To develop our faith muscles, we must take actual steps of faith.
During most of the year, the Jordan River was about 100 feet wide, but it became a mile wide at flood stage each spring. That was just when Israel crossed it (see Josh. 3). The water stopped flowing and stood like a wall about twenty miles upstream as soon as the priests bearing the ark put their feet into it. Unlike the crossing of the Red Sea (Exod. 14), this crossing wasn't brought about by the obedient arm of a leader (Moses' raised staff) but by the obedient feet of the people. It was God's miracle in response to faith.

Unless we're willing to "get our feet wet" by stepping in faith, we won't make much progress in the Christian life (cf. Matt 14:22-34).

DEEPENING YOUR DEVOTION TO GOD

Like the Israelites crossing the Jordan in uncharted territory, when we take steps of faith toward God's leading—despite our fears of drowning—we find Him faithful to make us "stand firm on dry ground in the middle of the Jordan" (Josh 3:17). And as Peter's example teaches us, we must *keep* our eyes on Him to stay afloat (Matt 14:30; Heb 12:2)! True faith acts.

Note the verbs in Hebrews 11: "offered…warned…built…went…lived…spoke…conquered," etc. Living faith is not mere intellectual assent to certain facts, but holistically embracing truth so that it leads to action (e.g., Jas 2:14-26). We can't arrogantly presume that *our* plans are God's plans (Jas 4:13-17), but we can know with certainty that our Shepherd will not ask us to go where He will not lead us (Josh 1:1-7; Psalm 23; John 10:1-18). You *can* trust Him: "Oh yes, you can! Thousands have."

For Discussion: How can you develop stronger faith muscles this year? How can you start by "getting your feet wet" for Christ today?

Family Activity: Make a sign that reads "O yes, you can! Thousands have," and discuss its implication for faithfully following God (cf. 1 Peter 5:9).

Day 10 – Faith

The Other Side of Faith

"The world was not worthy of them." –Heb 11:38a (NIV)

Before we move on from Hebrews 11, let's mine just a couple more of the abundant gems that sparkle in its forty verses. "God did it for me and I know He'll do it for you!" Have you ever heard somebody claim that? They can be *dangerous* words! They imply that God always works the same way in every situation, even though His plan and purpose may vary from person to person. God always honors faith (e.g., v. 6), but we must permit Him to honor it His way (e.g., Rom 9:20).

Heb 11:35-38 (please read), focuses on some winners who might appear to be losers. After all, they suffered for their faith and did not experience miraculous escapes like other faithful followers in chapter 11. Did they fail God? Did God fail them? No! It's just that these unnamed heroes glorified God *through* their suffering rather than by their escaping. And in doing so, they teach us more about living a life of faith in God.

The Life of Faith Is Costly – Those mentioned earlier in chapter 11 certainly paid a price for their faith. Abel gave up his life, Abraham left his home and family, Moses forfeited the treasures and pleasures of Egypt, and David was persecuted by Saul. Yet as we scan the closing verses of the chapter, we encounter new vocabulary: "tortured, refused to be released…jeers and flogging…chained and put in prison…stoned…sawed in two…put to death by the sword…destitute, persecuted and mistreated."

DEEPENING YOUR DEVOTION TO GOD

Like everything worthwhile, faith costs (though never as much as disbelief!). We must stand ready to be like Daniel's three friends on their way into Nebuchadnezzar's fiery furnace: "the God we serve is able to save us from it…. But even if he does not, we want you to know, O king, that we will not serve your gods" (Dan 3:16-17).

The Life of Faith Is Commended – From a human viewpoint, these "faith fanatics" were miserable failures. From the divine perspective, however, they were so precious that "the world was not worthy of them" (11:38). In essence, they were such magnificent specimens of faithfulness that they were *too* good to remain in such a wicked world! "These were all commended for their faith" and have a heavenly reward—one awaiting *all* people of faith (vv. 2, 16, 26, 35, 39-40).

Like an athlete, sometimes we collect scars before we collect medals (1 Cor 9:24-27; 2 Tim 2:3-5). Let us shun "fantastic faith formulas" and instead embrace the cost *and* the commendation of godly faith!

For Discussion: What steps of faith would make the world a little less worthy of you?

MEET ME IN THE MORNING

Day 11 – Faith

Tasty Faith

"Oh, taste and see that the LORD is good; Blessed is the man who trusts in Him!" –Psalm 34:8 (NKJ)

Once again we were at a stalemate. "I don't like it, it doesn't taste good!" Encouragement, anger, modeling, discipline, even downright manipulation. Nothing would do the trick. My oldest son was *not* going to eat his cranberry sauce! If I had taken a picture, I could show you a rigid case of lock jaw. "Should I get more drastic? Maybe if he sits there all night. Or goes hungry all day," I mused. Nope…it wasn't going to happen!

I had almost given up hope, when one day Lance finally gave in and ate some cranberry sauce. My wife and I held our breath. When he asked meekly for seconds, there was a spontaneous eruption of celebration around our dinner table. What was tantamount to torture for him instantly became a source of delight. My kids still laugh when we talk about the red "Thanksgiving Turkey Sauce."

What happened? First, Lance made a decision—however reluctantly—to open his mouth and taste it. Despite his doubts and fears, he moved toward something that he was told was good and good for him.

Second, my wife's patience had eventually won out. She had steadily encouraged Lance to eat foods that he initially balked at but ended up enjoying. Lance learned to trust her word—her warm invitation—and he was "blessed" in the process.

DEEPENING YOUR DEVOTION TO GOD

I wonder if we're, by faith, experiencing as much of God's goodness as we could be. Faithlessness says to God, "Who you are and what you want is not what I want. My lips are sealed. I won't even try." A fledgling faith says, "Lord, you promise to bless those who trust you. I will taste (move towards) you to experience your goodness, even though I have reservations." An experienced faith says, "God, I know you are good, even though the smell, feel, and unfamiliarity of this situation makes me recoil. I have tasted of your goodness and been blessed by trusting you before. Let's eat!" Even when everything looks bad, God is good. You can trust Him.

And be certain of this: you'll be nourished and satisfied when "you have tasted that the Lord is good" (1 Pet 2:3).

For Discussion: What are some ways you have tasted God's goodness when you trusted Him? If you can't think of any, are you ready to "open up?"

Family Activity: Sing the song "Lord, you are good and your mercy endured forever...." Then enjoy a sweet treat as you reflect on the ways God has been good to your family. (Cranberry Sauce is optional!)

MEET ME IN THE MORNING

Day 12 – Faith

Leaning Your Weight

"Jesus said to her, 'I am the resurrection and the life; he who believes in me will live even if he dies, and everyone who lives and believes in me will never die. Do you believe [in] this?" –John 11:25-26 (NAS)

Translating the ancient biblical languages in a way that communicates to a contemporary audience without distorting the original meaning is a complex process. Linguists, scholars, pastors, and theologians have long wrestled with this discipline. One man, John Paton is an under-celebrated missionary of great faithfulness. Paton dreamed of missions since early childhood. After studying theology and medicine, he was ordained by the Presbyterian Church and set sail to establish a church in a place called New Hebrides. Shortly after arriving on the island of Tanna, Paton's young wife died, followed by their infant son. For three more years, Paton labored alone to make Christ known among the hostile islanders. Although he barely escaped alive, the experience transformed his understanding of faith from a passive to an active concept.

Later, Paton returned and spent fifteen years on another island without any Christian witness. Paton was working one day in his hut on the translation of John's Gospel, puzzling over John's favorite expression *pisteuo eis*, to "believe in" or "to trust in." "How can I translate it?" he pondered. The islanders were cannibals; nobody trusted anybody. There wasn't even a word for "trust" or "faith" in their language! His native hireling came in. "What am I doing?" Paton asked him. "Sitting at your desk," the man replied. Paton then raised both feet off the floor and leaned back on his chair. "What am I doing now?" In reply, Paton's servant used a verb that means "to lean your whole weight upon." That's the phrase Paton wisely used throughout John's Gospel to convey faithful belief in God.

Our faith never stands alone; it always leans upon something or someone else. There's only One fully worthy of being that object, for only He "is able to keep you from falling and to make you stand before His glorious presence without fault and with great joy" (Jude 1:24)!

For Discussion: Have each person finish this statement and record the answers in your journal (Appendix E): "The area in my life right now where I most need to lean confidently upon God is..." Pray for faith.

Family Activity: Go around your home/yard and think up a few illustrations of belief. As you do them, relate the activity to the area you identified in the discussion.

Day 13 – Faith

Faith's Final Exam

"And Stephen, a man full of faith and power, did great wonders and signs among the people." –Acts 6:8 (NKJ)

How do you recognize priceless people? Just look at their price tags! To know what someone is worth, notice what it takes to buy them off. I wonder how you and I would do if we had to face "faith's final exam." It is an exam that more than a few Christians have had to face. It's a soul searching test with only one right answer.

Stephen, "a man full of faith and of the Holy Spirit" (Acts 6:6), faced this grueling test when "some men…rose up and argued with Stephen…and dragged him away" (vv. 9-12). They "looked intently at Stephen" as they hurled false charges against him in hopes of instigating his execution. Rather than capitulate to the pressure and deny his faith—even when given the chance (7:1)—he was fortified by faith and delivered one of the most impassioned speeches in the Bible (vv. 2-53).

(Incidentally, that this speech contains such a massive amount of accurate biblical data indicates that his faith was firmly founded on God's Word.) His speech wasn't well received! In fact, "when they heard this, they were furious and gnashed their teeth at him…they all rushed at him, dragged him out of the city and began to stone him" (vv. 54-58).

Faith's final exam is simply this: "Am I willing to die for what I believe?" We often sing about giving our all—even our life—to the Lord. But what if stones were actually being hurled at us? It's hard to conceive but important to contemplate, because our attitude about dying for our faith has much to say about how we'll live our faith!

Stephen was a priceless person who would not shrink back in his faith no matter how intense the threat was. This made him the first Christian martyr, although other ancient saints before him were "put to death" for their faith (Heb 11:35-39). While we pray that our families will never face that, may we also be able to confidently say with Paul at the end of our life, whenever that might be, "I have kept the faith" (2 Tim 4:7)!

For Discussion: How do you think you might answer faith's final exam?

Family Activity: Make up "price tags" for some things in your home. Let the kids guess how much those things are worth before you tell them.

Next, ask them to put a price tag on a Bible, then themselves. Remind them of the incalculable value of Scripture, their life, and faith.

Sacrifice

Memory Verse:
"But just as you excel in everything—in faith, in speech, in knowledge, in complete earnestness and in your love for us—see that you also excel in this grace of giving." 2 Corinthians 8:7 (NIV)

Reading through the NT in 40 Days

- John 11-16 .... Day 14
- John 17-22 .... Day 15
- Acts 1-5 .... Day 16
- Acts 6-11 .... Day 17
- Acts 12-17 .... Day 18
- Acts 18-23 .... Day 19
- Acts 24-28 .... Day 20

"The only thing most of us know about 'sacrifice' is how to spell the word!" – Jacob Stam

Day 14 – Sacrifice

Spiritual Sacrifices – Part One

"You also, like living stones, are being built into a spiritual house to be a holy priesthood, offering spiritual sacrifices acceptable to God through Jesus Christ." –1 Peter 2:5 (NIV)

Many Christians have discarded the concept of offering God sacrifices as bloody, antiquated rituals with no modern relevance. But relegating sacrifices exclusively to another era has weakened the gravity and urgency of many central facets of the Christian life. Certainly, Jesus is the perfect once-for-all sacrifice for our sins and we are not bound to the Old Testament (OT) Levitical system (e.g., Heb. 5-10). As "a holy priesthood," however, we *are* called to offer "spiritual sacrifices" (1 Pet 2:5).

Among those are the following:

A Sacrifice of Speaking – "Through Him, then let us continually offer up a sacrifice of praise to God, that is, the fruit of lips that give thanks to His name" (Heb 13:15; cf. 12:28 NAS). Using OT language (e.g., Ps 50:14, 23; Hos 14:2), we're told to offer praise sacrifices from our lips instead of fruit crops from our fields. In fact, the reason you're part of the "royal priesthood" is so "that you may declare the praises of him who called you out of darkness into his wonderful light" due to His great "mercy" (1 Pet 2:9-10). Has your mouth made a sacrifice today?

A Sacrifice of Sharing – Since thankful praise is expressed with our lives as much as our lips, the next verse reads: "And do not forget to do good and to share with others, for with such sacrifices God is pleased" (Heb 13:16). Material sacrifice is no longer what we use to burn on the altar but what we use to bless another. God is happy when we selflessly sacrifice for others (cf. Matt 9:13; 12:7). Do you sacrifice by sharing?

A Sacrifice of Serving – In Phil 2:17 and 2 Tim 4:6, Paul adopts another image from the OT sacrificial ritual; namely, "being poured out like a drink offering." Certain OT sacrifices featured wine being ceremonially poured out (e.g., Num 15:1-10). When Paul used the expression, it referred to willingly giving himself to serve others at great personal cost. It's a sacrifice worth making. Are you?

A Sacrifice of Supplication – Because we have "a great high priest…Jesus," we no longer need a human order of priests to mediate between God and people as in the OT (e.g., Joel 2:17; Mal 1:9). Instead, we can ourselves "approach the throne of grace with confidence," offering prayer sacrifices to God (Heb 4:14-16; cf. Rev 8:3-5). Are you seizing this privilege?

For Discussion: How does or should viewing the above acts as a personal sacrifice to God affect your thinking about them?

Day 15 – Sacrifice

Spiritual Sacrifices – Part Two

"[Jesus] has made us to be a kingdom and priests to serve his God and Father." –Revelation 1:6 (NIV)

Since we "have been made to be...priests to serve our God" (Rev 5:10) in Jesus' "permanent priesthood" (Heb 7:24), we're privileged to offer many priestly sacrifices. Picking up yesterday's discussion, let's reflect on more spiritual sacrifices that God delights in today.

A Sacrifice of Self – No longer do God's people offer dead plants and animals to Him. Instead, we're urged "to offer your bodies as living sacrifices, holy and pleasing to God—this is your spiritual act of worship" (Rom 12:1). The word "offer" had a technical meaning for presenting a sacrifice. Here, it's presenting our very bodies to and for God.

A Sacrifice of Separation – Our ongoing self-sacrifice involves separation from the world's standards and transformation "by the renewing of [our] mind" (Rom 12:2). Moreover, in the context of being a *holy* priesthood who offer spiritual sacrifices (1 Pet 2:5, 9), we learn to separate ourselves from sin (v. 1) unto God (v. 4) and as "aliens and strangers to abstain from fleshly lusts which wage war against the soul" (v. 11). Sacrifices of submission (vv. 13-18) and suffering (vv. 19-25) follow suit.

A Sacrifice of Support – The striking sacrificial language in Phil 4:18 describe generous financial support of ministry: "I have received...the gifts you sent. They are a fragrant offering, an acceptable sacrifice, pleasing to God." At this time only the Philippians alone sacrificed for Paul's ministry (v. 15). And they did it repeatedly—even when he was serving in cities far wealthier than their own (v. 16). They not only gained a heavenly reward (v. 17), but since they apparently gave to the point of being in need themselves, they obtained the assurance for all who give generously: "And my God will meet all your needs according to his glorious riches in Christ Jesus" (v. 19).

A Sacrifice of Salvation – Like Paul, we should view ourselves as "a minister of Christ Jesus…with the priestly duty of proclaiming the gospel of God, so that the [converts] might become an offering acceptable to God" (Rom 15:16). Here we learn that both the proclamation and product of that proclamation—new believers—are pleasing sacrifices to God! Have you made such an offering lately?

To Discuss and Do: Brainstorm how Christians can make sacrifices in each area introduced the last two days. Decide together to offer a specific spiritual sacrifice that aligns with one or more categories. Then, do it!

Day 16 – Sacrifice

Generous Grace Giving

"But just as you excel in everything—in faith, in speech, in knowledge, in complete earnestness and in your love for us—see that you also excel in this grace of giving." –2 Corinthians 8:7 (NIV)

If you're like me, you can become satisfied by legitimate progress in certain areas of the Christian life while remaining stubbornly stagnant in other areas. If Paul were telling Saint Paul's Baptist Church that we excelled in the virtues of 2 Cor 8:7a—and we ardently strive to, we'd probably feel a certain sense of justified satisfaction. But as important as those qualities are, they're incomplete without affecting one of the most important parts of our lives—our finances. And so, Paul exhorts abundant giving as both a virtue and an expression of other virtues. His encouragement for financial generosity as an "act of grace" (v. 6) is bolstered by at least three motivations (read 2 Cor. 8).

The Grace of God – "The grace that God has given the Macedonian churches" (v. 1) compelled them to "well up in rich generosity… even beyond their ability" (vv. 2-3). God's grace is powerfully manifest in Saint Paul's! Will we likewise "well up" (overflow) in grace-giving? By definition, we can't earn grace. But we certainly can *respond lavishly to it*!

The Church of God – Since compelling examples can stimulate our imagination, Paul highlighted the Macedonians' generosity. After all, "they urgently pleaded…for the privilege of sharing in this service [of giving] to the saints" (v. 4), despite their "extreme poverty" (v. 2). Because "they gave themselves first to the Lord"

(v. 5), their "earnestness" is a worthy comparison for "the sincerity of [our] love" (v. 8). Saint Paul's has a great opportunity right now to *be* like the ancient church, *bless* the contemporary church, and *build* the future church. Will you sacrifice to be a part of this "privilege of sharing?"

The Son of God – Why else should we abound in giving? Because someone else did so for us in an even greater way: "For you know the grace of our Lord Jesus Christ, that though he was rich, yet for your sakes he became poor, so that you through his poverty might become rich" (v. 9). Does your giving show your gratitude to Christ and reflect His image (Rom 8:28-30; Eph 4:11-16; 2 Cor 5:15)?

For Discussion: What prevents people from "excelling in this grace of giving," and how does the truth above affect those reasons?

Family Activity: Think of the most generous people you know. Come up with several questions and conduct a mini-interview with one person to learn more about being generous.

MEET ME IN THE MORNING

Day 17 – Sacrifice

Pass the Fries

"Everything in heaven and earth is yours... Wealth and honor come from you... and we have given you only what comes from your hand... all of it belongs to you." –1 Chronicles 29:11-16 (NIV)

For little guys, my children were pretty impressive at sharing. But like their daddy, they're certainly not perfect. I remember several days treating them to lunch at McDonalds. Not being very hungry for their gourmet cuisine, I ordered "Super Size Fries" for my kids and planned to bum a few from them. However, when I reached over on one occasion to grab my youngest son's fries, he handed me one shriveled fry and snatched the rest away.

Typically I would laugh and he would grin and we'd dig in. But this time a wave of "righteous indignation" hit me. "He's teasing me! How can he not share a portion of my bountiful gift? Doesn't he know that if I hadn't provided these he'd have no fries, not to mention far more than usual? How dare he be so selfish with my blessing!"

God must have wanted to reteach me something, because I soon sensed His raised eyebrow looking at me. As I drove away, it dawned on me that my son behaved the way I'm tempted to act toward God. He gives so freely out of His bountiful wealth. In fact, He's graciously chosen to give me so much more than I deserve—and certainly more than I need. And what do I do? To be honest, there've been times I selfishly hoarded His gifts. Other times I've offered back just a taste, a tease, and gotten fat on the rest. Sad, huh? Can you ever relate?

DEEPENING YOUR DEVOTION TO GOD

I'm not just referring to money, of course, but this incident reminded me of a conversation I heard of between a one- and a fifty-dollar bill. The dollar said, "Hey, where ya been? Haven't seen you much." The fifty answered exuberantly, "I've been hanging out at casinos and fancy restaurants. Just got back from a cruise and a resort. How 'bout you?" The one dollar bill replied meekly, "You know, same old stuff—church, church, church." Money talks…but *God's* money should never talk *that* way!

David's prayer at the dedication of offerings to fund the new temple (see verses above) helps me realign my priorities. How about you?

For Discussion: How is your willingness to give affected by knowing that: (1) God owns everything, (2) every good gift is from Him (Matt 7:11; Jas 1:17), and (3) what we give is from Him to start with?

Family Activity: Have each decide to share something special—any blessing from God—with someone else, even if they don't deserve it!

Day 18 – Sacrifice

Heavenly Treasure

"Do not store up for yourselves treasures on earth, where moth and rust destroy, and where thieves break in and steal. But store up for yourselves treasures in heaven." –Matthew 6:19-20a (NAS)

Before Jim Elliot was murdered by the Aouka Indians in Ecuador with whom he was trying to share Christ, he had written in his journal this now widely circulated saying: "He is no fool who gives that which he can not keep, in order to gain that which he cannot lose."

Jesus would agree with Elliot's words. In Matthew 6, He warns against accumulating possessions simply to greedily hoard them or spend them selfishly on undue extravagance. As those whom God expects not to love the world or anything in the world (1 John 2:15), we're to expunge from our lives "greed, which is idolatry" (Col 3:5).

In the Ancient Orient, wealth was basically preserved in three ways: (1) garments (e.g., Judg 14:12), which could be destroyed by moths; (2) grain (e.g., Luke 12:18), which could be devoured by rodents, worms, and vermin (the word translated "rust" literally means "eating"); and (3) gold or precious metals, which thieves could steal. In other words, the Lord presents the totality of wealth as a passing commodity that we aren't to stockpile. And even if they are preserved here, they can't go with us into eternity (Luke 16:19-31). Have *you* ever seen a U-haul behind a hearse?!

DEEPENING YOUR DEVOTION TO GOD

Jesus does not advocate poverty. The one time He told a person to "sell your possessions and give to the poor" (Matt 19:21) was because that young man's wealth was a barrier between him and the lordship of Christ. To honestly and prudently earn, save, invest, and spend is wise. But we can't love or hoard the things of this world. Instead, we must hold them lightly, realizing that Heaven is the only safe place for our treasure. If our heart is there, our treasure will also be (Matt 6:21).

Paul tells Christians not "to put their hope in wealth, which is so uncertain, but to put their hope in God, who richly provides us with everything for our enjoyment…be rich in good deeds, and to be generous and willing to share. In this way they will lay up treasure for themselves as a firm foundation for the coming age" (1 Tim 6:17-19). Invest in eternity…send it ahead now!

For Discussion: Are you selfishly hoarding earthly possessions? What does God want you to do instead? What does your treasure say about your heart? What can you store in heaven this week?

Day 19 – Sacrifice

Sow and Grow

"Whoever sows sparingly will also reap sparingly, and whoever sows generously will also reap generously." –2 Corinthians 9:6 (NIV)

To the uninitiated, basketball appears to be a rather disorganized sport. Everyone runs up and down the court, back and forth in circles and sprints. They do, however, have plays. One of the few that I personally understand from other sports is the "give and go." You give someone the ball and then you go toward the basket. They pass back to you, and you shoot. Let me suggest a play that we desperately need to execute more often in our lives: the "give and grow!"

In 2 Corinthians 9, we're encouraged to sow generously for the prosperity of other people (vv. 1-5, 12), the provision of our needs (vv. 8-10), and the praise of God (vv. 11-15). Its simple mathematics: sparingly = sparingly; bountifully = bountifully. Its rudimentary agriculture: if you plant a lot of seed, you can expect a large harvest…and vice-versa. Which would you rather have? As families we can sow with our time (daily and periodic investments), talents (the gifts, skills, and abilities God's given us), treasure (financial and material resources), testimony (the story of God's grace and power in our lives), and temple (the bodies God has blessed us with). That's a lot of material to execute the "give and grow!"

Paul says that generous sowers "will be made rich in every way so that [they] can be generous on every occasion" (v. 11a). What an eye-opener! Our wealth isn't given primarily to expand our

DEEPENING YOUR DEVOTION TO GOD

luxury but to enable our generosity. Everything that God has given you (and that's everything you have!) is a divinely ordained opportunity for sacrificial sharing. We should all have a supply of stickers that read, "Opportunity!" Imagine placing them on everything God puts in our lives: our house, paycheck, car, business, etc. Each thing is an opportunity to express faith, praise, love, kindness, and more.

As we come to expect in Scripture, there's a reward for seizing these opportunities, a bountiful harvest—whether here or in heaven (cf. Luke 6:38). Although we don't "give to get," with such lavish compensation, isn't it time we stop asking, "How much should I give?" and start asking instead, "How much should I *keep*?" Even when it's tough, "Let us not become weary in doing good, for at the proper time we will reap a harvest if we do not give up" (Gal 6:7-9)!

For Discussion: Have you grown by giving (the "give and grow")?

Family Activity: Write "Opportunity!" on several post-it notes, discuss its meaning, and put them around the house, on yourselves, etc.

Day 20 – Sacrifice

Worthless Worry

"…do not worry…" –Matthew 6:25, 31, 34 (NKJ)

Jesus knows us so perfectly, doesn't He? He anticipates that His call to heavenly investment and serving God rather than money (Matt 6:19-24) will illicit all sorts of anxiety in us. Talk of sacrifice usually does that to us, doesn't it? So after addressing the accumulation of wealth, the Master discusses anxiety over wealth, so that we can live the generous God centered lives He desires (6:25-34).

Think of the thickest fog you've ever seen. According to an article I read, dense fog covering seven city blocks 100 feet deep is composed of less than one gallon of water. It only takes a few gallons to cripple a city or cause crashes on country roads! People drive cautiously, seldom daring even the routine risks that accompany their normal driving patterns.

Worry over wealth and wellness is a lot like that. "What if I don't hoard more possessions for myself? What if I give *too* much?" Just a smattering can cripple our thinking and harm our life. It chokes our generosity. Someone has said, "Worry is a thin stream of fear that trickles through the mind, which, if encouraged, will cut a channel so wide that all other thoughts will be drained out."

Although anxiety is a part of life for all of us, let's recognize what message obsessive worrying sends to God: "I know you mean well when you say you'll take care of me, but I'm not sure you can pull it off." Worry is distrusting God's promises, power, providence, protection and provision.

Worry is futile (vv. 25-27), faithless (vv. 28-30), acting Fatherless (vv. 31-32), and ultimately fruitless (vv. 33-34). And even though we can't change the past, we can ruin a perfectly good present by worrying about the future.

God beckons us to trust Him to take care of us as we serve Him as our Master and seek to put His kingdom priorities first in our lives (vv. 24, 26, 30, 32-33). When that is our aim, then how we view, pursue, and use our resources will show it. Peace will follow prayer when we petition God (Phil 4:6-7), so "cast all your anxiety on him because he cares for you" (1 Pet 5:7)!

To Do and Discuss: Read and reread Matthew 6:25-34 slowly and in more than one version (if available). Then write these labels in your journal (Appendix E): arguments against worrying, assurances that prevent worrying, and alternatives to worrying. List, discuss, and apply insights from this text.

Purpose

Memory Verse:
"For it is God who works in you to will and to act according to his good purpose." - Philippians 2:13 (NIV)

Reading through the NT in 40 Days

- Romans 1-8 .... Day 21
- Romans 9-16 .... Day 22
- 1 Corinthians 1-8 .... Day 23
- 1 Corinthians 9-16 .... Day 24
- 2 Corinthians 1-6 .... Day 25
- 2 Corinthians 7-13 .... Day 26
- Galatians .... Day 27

"Purpose: the reason for which something exists or is done, made, etc.; an intended or desired result; aim; goal."
–Webster's Dictionary

MEET ME IN THE MORNING

Day 21 – Purpose

The Main Thing

"So, whether you eat or drink, or whatever you do, do everything for the glory of God." –1 Corinthians 10:31 (NIV)

When the Crystal Palace Exhibition opened in 1851, people flocked to London's Hyde Park to behold its many inventions. One of the greatest marvels back then was steam. On display were steam plows, locomotives, looms, organs—even a steam cannon. Of all the great exhibits that year, the first prize winner was a steam invention with an amazing 7000 moving parts. When it was turned on, it came alive with pulleys, whistles, bells, and gears. It made a lot of noise, but ironically it didn't do a thing.

Seven thousand moving parts caused a lot of commotion, but they served no purpose! In our high tech era, it's easy to confuse activity with purposefulness. We can be lulled into believing that the noise of gears and pulleys is the sound of something worthwhile. This can be as true for a church as it can for a person…having 1000s of moving parts making a lot of noise but accomplishing little of God's purposes.

In the last five years, Saint Paul's has defined and refined its purpose, mission, vision, and core values. They help keep us purposeful with the flurry of activity our church enjoys. We recognize, however, that above it all, driving all we do is "the main thing." What is that fundamental reason for our existence and activity? Glorifying God!

DEEPENING YOUR DEVOTION TO GOD

Our overriding mandate, aspiration, and expectation is for God to be glorified in our church, our lives, our everything (e.g., Ps 73:24-28; 86:8-12; Matt 5:16; John 12:28; 1 Cor 6:20; 10:31; Phil 1:11; 2:11; 2 Thess. 1:11-12; 1 Pet 4:1; Rev 4:11; 5:12). We must aim to magnify and elevate God. We need to put Him and His priorities in first place, where He can shine on the center stage of all we are and do. The activities are limitless, but the purpose is constant. So let's remember that the main thing is to keep the main thing the main thing, "so that with one heart and mouth [we] may glorify the God and Father of our Lord Jesus Christ" (Rom 15:6)!

For Discussion: Brainstorm the normal activities in your life and consider how you can practically glorify God in each of those things?

Family Activity: Take your kids on a tour of the house, stopping at various items like your phone, table, computer, car, etc. Consider together, "How can or should we use this to glorify God?"

Day 22 – Purpose

Can't Do It Alone

"For it is God who works in you to will and to act according to his good purpose." –Philippians 2:13 (NIV)

"I can't do it alone!" Many of us are conditioned to automatically hear that admission as a cry of weakness. As Christians, however, we should recognize its honest value. Indeed, from the beginning we were "sinful at birth" (Ps 51:5), "darkened in [our] understanding and separated from the life of God" (Eph 4:18)," and "powerless" (Rom 5:6) to do anything of godly, eternal value in our own strength (Rom 3:8-20; cf. Isa 34:6; 1 Cor. 2:14). Ouch!

The good news is that "because of his great love for us, God, who is rich in mercy, made us alive with Christ even when we were dead in transgressions" (Eph 2:5). Now, we are no longer "under the control of the evil one" (1 John 5:19), but "able to test and approve what God's will is" (Rom 12:2). That ability is critical, because in Phil 2:12 Paul urges his "beloved" (i.e., believers in Christ) to "continue to work out [not *for*!] our own salvation." Nothing we have, are, or do can earn God's gift of salvation (e.g., Eph 2:8-9). But once God has saved us, we're told to "work out" what He has "worked in" us, according to the pattern of Christ's unselfish humility and sacrificial obedience (Phil 2:5-11).

Given the daily battle we wage with our fleshly desires (e.g., Gal 5:16-26; 1 Pet 2:12), it's profoundly encouraging that God hasn't left us to "do it alone." We'd fail miserably! Instead, He "works in you" to bring about two inseparable facets of a God-glorifying life: (1) wanting His good purposes to be realized, and (2) working in alignment with those purposes.

God's permanent residence within us (e.g., John 14:23; 1 Cor 6:19-20) is an internal combustion engine energizing us to desire and do just what He wants! We couldn't accomplish our own salvation, but He's empowering us to accomplish His own purposes. He has the power, the place ("in you"), and the purpose (cf. Heb 13:21). Will you join Him?!

For Discussion: Describe a spiritual accomplishment that you can directly attribute to God's empowerment of your will (desiring) and working (doing). What lessons can be learned from that?

Family Activity: Ask the kid(s) to decide on a project they can't do alone but could accomplish with the whole family's combined strength. As you do it together, discuss why and how God helps us do what He wants. "I can't. He can. We will!"

Day 23 – Purpose

Big Rocks

"Therefore be careful how you walk, not as unwise men but as wise, making the most of your time, because the days are evil."
–Eph 5:15-16 (NAS)

God's purposes for the church are also His purposes for our lives. In summary, you were planned for God's pleasure (worshipping God), formed for God's family (fellowshipping with other believers), created to become like Christ (spiritual growth as a disciple), shaped for serving God (ministry to insiders in the Body Christian), and made for a mission (sharing your life and faith with outsiders).

God wants us to integrate each of these purposes into our daily lives. But how do we do it all? An illustration used by a time management expert can help. As he stood before a group of overachieving business students, he pulled out a one-gallon, wide-mouthed Mason jar. Setting it on the table, he took about a dozen fist-sized rocks and carefully placed them into the jar one at a time.

When no more rocks would fit inside, he asked, "Is the jar full?" Everyone replied, "Yes." So he pulled out a hidden bucket of gravel and dumped some in. He shook the jar, causing pieces to work themselves down into the spaces between the big rocks. "Is it full now?" he asked. By now the class was on to him. "Probably not," one answered. "Good!" he replied.

Reaching under the table for another bucket, he dumped in

sand, which went into all the spaces between the rocks and gravel. Once more he asked, "Is this jar full?" "No!" they shouted. "Good!" he said, as he grabbed a pitcher of water and poured it in until the jar was filled to the brim. The point *isn't* that no matter how full your schedule is you can always fit more into it!

The moral is: *If you don't put the big rocks in first, you'll never get them in at all!* Although they cover every area of our lives, Scripture says that the five purposes above are the only really "big rocks" in our lives. Let's be wise people who make the most of our time by filling it with the big rocks first (Eph 5:15-21)!

For Discussion: What do each of these five purposes mean? How do, could, or should you prioritize them in your life (By the way, if you missed the year's campaign, copies of Rick Warren's book The Purpose-Driven Life are available in Charisma).

Family Activity: Think up a version of the illustration above. Label your "big rocks" with God's purposes for your lives. Talk about how to prioritize these purposes as you fill up your "jar" with life's "other stuff."

Day 24 – Purpose

The "E-Church"

"They were continually devoting themselves to the apostles' teaching and to fellowship, to the breaking of bread and to prayer....They were...praising God...And the Lord was adding to their number day by day those who were being saved." –Acts 2:42, 47 (NAS)

In our electronic age, "e" must feel like king of the alphabet! We have email for communicating, e-books for reading, e-Bay for shopping, e-Trade for investing, even e-Harmony for dating. But long before this recent phenomenon, God wanted us to have an "e-church"!

Using that tireless letter "e" and the example of the first church in Acts 2, let's briefly consider God's purposes for the local church—the major ways we carry out our main purpose of glorifying God. And since we, the people, *are* the church, these purposes for us corporately will also be the purposes for us as individuals and families.

Exalt the Lord – The new church was characterized by devotion to "prayer," "the breaking of bread" (likely the ordinance of communion, showing Christ's centrality), and "praising God" (vv. 42d, 47). God's people are worshipping people in as many ways as possible!

Edify and Educate Believers – The early band of believers "were continually devoting themselves to the apostles' teaching" (v. 42a). God's people are immersed in God's Word, plain and simple!

DEEPENING YOUR DEVOTION TO GOD

Expunge Sin from Our Lives – "Those who accepted [Peter's Gospel] message were baptized" (v. 41), a picture of the cleansing of sin from our lives (e.g., Rom 6:1-14). God's people are holy people!

Equip and Enrich the Saints for Ministry – The early Christians in Jerusalem didn't waste any time learning to minister sacrificially and joyfully (vv. 43-46). After all, God's people are serving people!

Exchange our Lives in Fellowship – Their devotion to "fellowship" (v. 42) showed up in many remarkable ways (read vv. 44-46). God's people are sharing people, even at personal expense!

Evangelize the Lost – As a result of all this purposefulness, the church was "enjoying the favor of all the people. And the Lord added to their number daily those who were being saved" (v. 47). God's people are witnessing people! Will you be a part of the "e-church?"

For Discussion: Discuss at least three ways that a larger and more functional facility will enable us to accomplish each of these purposes in greater quantity with greater quality and, therefore, greater glory for God.

MEET ME IN THE MORNING

Day 25 – Purpose

A Legacy of Purpose

"For when David had served God's purpose in his own generation, he fell asleep." –Acts 13:36a (NIV)

Toward the end of the 19th century, Swedish chemist Alfred Nobel awoke one morning to read his own obituary in the local newspaper: "Alfred Nobel, the inventor of dynamite, who died yesterday, devised a way for more people to be killed in a war than ever before, and he died a very rich man." Can you imagine him reading that about himself? A newspaper reporter had bungled the epitaph. It was actually Alfred's older brother who had died!

Still, reading that account had a profound effect on Nobel. He immediately decided he wanted to be known for something other than developing ways to kill people efficiently and for amassing a fortune in the process. So he initiated the Nobel Peace Prize, which has become the supreme award given to those who have—in the opinion of the givers—made an exceptional contribution to the world's peace and betterment. Because of the unique opportunity to read his own obituary in his lifetime, Nobel isn't remembered as a merchant of death and destruction but as a man of charity and peace.

If you were to pass on soon, how do you think *your* obituary would read?

Wouldn't it be great if we could all make mid-course corrections to alter the outcome of our legacy? Actually, we can! Just as

Nobel's confrontation with the ugly truth about himself led to a new and improved life purpose, so King David's understanding of his sin and shortcomings led to fresh resolve to accomplish God's will in his day (cf. 2 Sam. 12 with Ps. 51). By the end, David had earned what are perhaps the best descriptions of a life well-lived. Paul was able to say: "For when David had served God's purpose in his own generation, he fell asleep" (i.e., died; Acts 13:36).

More importantly, the Lord Himself had said: "I have found David the son of Jesse, a man after my own heart, who will do all my will" (v. 22). These historical footnotes comprise one of the most honorable epitaphs imaginable—living a life consumed with God's purposes in the generation He has placed us. May that be able to be said of Saint Paul's and each of us when God calls us home!

For Discussion: What do you hope people could truthfully and confidently say about you when you die? What must happen for that to be said?

MEET ME IN THE MORNING

Day 26 – Purpose

Giant Icebergs

"So then do not be foolish, but understand what the will of the Lord is."
–Ephesians 5:17 (NAS)

If you fly over the North Atlantic Ocean, you will see awesome icebergs floating in those frigid waters. If you look carefully, you'll notice a pattern develop: small icebergs move in one direction, while gigantic icebergs move in another. Why does this happen? Because the surface winds drive the small icebergs, while deep and powerful ocean currents control the large ones.

There is a lesson in this for us. Lives are driven by various forces. "Small lives" are driven to and fro by the surface winds of change, petty problems, disagreeable circumstances, self-centeredness, and the like (Eph 4:14). They are overwhelmed and disoriented by what whirls around, resulting in aimless drifting. On the other hand, "great lives" aren't detoured by the petty gusts of surface winds. Their foundations run deep in God's timeless purposes (cf. Col 3:16).

How are we sheltered from the whims of the surface winds and grounded in the strong currents of God's purpose? By understanding His eternal will and ordering our lives around it. There's no better place to start doing that than with the Bible verses that *explicitly* state that something is "the will of God," including being:

- Saved – Trusting in Jesus' work on the cross and accepting Him as your personal Forgiver and Leader (1 Tim 2:3-4; cf. 2 Pet 3:9).

DEEPENING YOUR DEVOTION TO GOD

- Spirit-Filled – Consistently yielding your life to the controlling influence of the Holy Spirit through the Word (Eph 5:17-18; cf. Gal 5:16, 25; Eph 4:30; Col 3:16; 1 Thess 5:19).

- Sanctified – Progressive separation from sin and transformation into Christ's image (1 Thess 4:3; cf. Rom 8:29-30; Eph 4:13-16).

- Submissive – Voluntarily and humbly aligning yourself under God and His appointed authorities (1 Pet 2:13-15; cf. 5:5-10; Rom 13:1-7; Eph 5:21-6:9; Heb 13:17).

- Suffering for His Sake – Accepting (temporary!) unpleasant consequences for doing right rather than suffering for doing wrong, which demonstrates Christ's lordship in your life (1 Pet 3:15-17).

- Saying Thanks – Being grateful to God in all circumstances, no matter how delightful or dismal (1 Thess 5:18; cf. Phil 4:4-7). Great lives are lived by those who are saved, Spirit-filled, sanctified, submissive, suffering, and saying thanks!

For Discussion: Look up at least the primary verse for each element of God's will and discuss how obeying that would make a "gigantic life."

Day 27 – Purpose

Give Me the Details

"It will be told you what you must do." –Ephesians 5:17 (NAS)

In Acts 9, a man named Ananias had an even more frightening assignment. The Lord said, "Go to the house of Judas on Straight Street and ask for a man from Tarsus named Saul" (v. 11). Ananias knew Saul's main priority was harassing the Christians and instigating their demise. I could imagine him not wanting to obey, but he went nonetheless. Do you know what he found when he got there? Jesus had already met Saul on the road to Damascus! Saul, renamed Paul, was simply waiting for someone to come and fill in the details about Jesus and what he should do next.

In Acts 10, the Lord told Peter to go to a Gentile army officer named Cornelius. Peter was so skeptical that God had to send a vision to convince him. Imagine the cultural gap. For a humble Jewish fisherman to go to the home of a leading Gentile army officer must have felt tenuous. But however reluctantly, Peter also obeyed. What do you think he found? Well, when he got there, he found that God had already been working in Cornelius' life. He and "a large gathering of people" (v. 27) had assembled and were eagerly waiting to hear Peter's message!

As you reflect on your life and listen for God's leading, can you identify an area of great need that lacks what God wants to offer through you? It's probably a person, group, or place that seems a bit overwhelming to reach. It may be somewhere or some group that—humanly speaking—is a bit "impractical and improbable" for you to minister to. Sacrifice is likely required.

DEEPENING YOUR DEVOTION TO GOD

Perhaps thinking about that your assignment frightens you a little—or a lot. But maybe that is just the purpose He has for you. You may find different results than those in Acts, but no matter how uncertain the situation, our Lord prepares the way and empowers us to accomplish His purpose, so ask God to give you the details now (cf. Isa 52:12; Phil 2:13; Eph 6:10)!

For Discussion: Read Matthew 9:35-38 and John 4:35. Then help each person or the whole family identify an area of need to which they can respond. How do the stories from Acts affect how you should relate to this need? Do you believe that God will go before you, as He did in these accounts from Acts (cf. Job 42:2; Prov 19:21)? If He chooses to act differently, how will or should that affect you? Pray for motivation and strength to begin or continue serving the Lord's purposes there...today!

Service

Memory Verse:
"Always give yourselves fully to the work of the Lord, because you know that your labor in the Lord is not in vain."
- *1 Corinthians 15:58b (NIV)*

Reading through the NT in 40 Days

- Ephesians .... Day 28
- Philippians – Colossians .... Day 29
- 1 – 2 Thessalonians .... Day 30
- 1 Timothy .... Day 31
- 2 Timothy – Philemon .... Day 32
- Hebrews 1-6 .... Day 33
- Hebrews 7-13 .... Day 34

"A non-ministering Christian is a contradiction in terms!"
–D. Elton Trueblood

Day 28 – Service

Your Calcutta

"The one who calls you is faithful and he will do it." –1 Thess 5:24 (NIV)

Many years ago, a young boy wrote an enthusiastic letter to Mother Teresa. In it, he asked her how he could make a difference with his life, like she had with hers. He waited. For months he didn't hear back. As he was giving up hope of receiving a reply, he got a letter from Calcutta, India, where Teresa had long served faithfully and purposefully. He expectantly opened it and read just four handwritten words that revolutionized his life: "Find your own Calcutta." What a challenge we should all heed! Talk about life purpose!

Okay, imagine that you're living in the following situation: You're in a country where Christians are a distinct and increasingly despised minority. The official state policy is decidedly anti-Christian. In fact, a systematic program of harassment, imprisonment, torture, and even execution is being carried out against believers. There are few "safe places" to find refuge. To complicate matters, your country has recently lost a war and is living under occupation by foreign troops. This foreign power is theoretically neutral about religion but fears the Christian minority may destabilize the situation. Like most other Christians, you're among the lower class with no political or economic clout. Are you getting the picture?

Now, as if just surviving weren't enough, the leader of your little band of Christians announces that you're going on an evangelistic visitation program. He hands you three assignments to choose from: (1) One is the secretary of the treasury of a powerful neighboring country who has been visiting your country for an economic conference. (2) The second is a leading official of the majority religion in your country. He is among those chiefly responsible for the increasingly brutal campaign against Christians. (3) The last name is one of the top officers of the occupying forces, a man known as a fair but tough administrator of the law. With whom would you choose to share the message and love of Christ?

If you survey the book of Acts, you'll find almost the identical situation I just described. In Acts 8, the Lord ordered the Christian Philip to go down into the Gaza strip and meet an important government official from Ethiopia who was sitting in his chariot reading. I could empathize if Philip was reluctant to go. But when he got there, he found this man actually reading from the book of Isaiah and contemplating whom the prophet was writing about. When Philip identified the subject of the passage as Jesus Christ, the man believed and was baptized on the spot!

Day 29 - Service

An Excuse to Serve

"May the God of peace… equip you with everything good for doing his will, and may he work in us what is pleasing to him."–Heb 13:20-21a (NIV)

Whenever somebody starts talking about Christian service, it's best to duck. Why? Because excuses will inevitably fly! We can think of a zillion reasons why we shouldn't begin to serve, continue serving, or step into greater ministry responsibilities. I've heard a lot, and even made a few myself. Fortunately, God gave us a BIG Bible. And the lives of the many remarkable servants in that book cover every category of excuse we could make for not being people who "serve the LORD with gladness" (Ps 100:2).

So if you're concerned that there are just too many reasons why you can't serve, you're in good company. Here is a sampling…

Moses stuttered.	John was self-righteous.
David's armor didn't fit.	Samson was "codependent."
Paul rejected John Mark.	Naomi was a widow.
Timid Timothy had ulcers.	Paul and Moses murdered.
Hosea's wife was a prostitute.	Jonah ran from God.
Amos was just a fig farmer.	Miriam was a gossip.
Joseph was abused.	Gideon and Thomas doubted.
Jacob lied and was insecure.	Jeremiah was depressed.
David had an affair.	Elijah was burned out.
Solomon was too rich.	Martha was a worrywart.
Jesus was too poor.	Mary was lazy.
Abraham was too old.	Samson had long hair.
David was too young.	Noah got drunk.

DEEPENING YOUR DEVOTION TO GOD

Peter was afraid of death.	Peter had a short fuse.
Lazarus was dead.	Zacchaeus was unpopular.
Habakkuk was impatient.	John the Baptist? Eccentric!

For all His gentleness, Jesus wasn't very sympathetic toward excuses (cf. Luke 14:16-35). Fortunately, Hudson Taylor was correct to say, "All God's giants were weak people." In fact, He chose "foolish" and "weak" people to serve Him, "so that no-one may boast before him" (1 Cor 1:27-29). On top of that He said, "My grace is sufficient for you, for my power is made perfect in weakness" (2 Cor 12:9). It is from a posture of "weakness" that we can serve in "power" (13:4). So let's stop making excuses for not serving—and start viewing each hindrance as an "excuse" to experience and serve in God's grace and power!

To Do and Discuss: Record a list of excuses you've made or heard for not serving. Then, cross each out as you discuss how each statement actually reveals an opportunity to experience God's grace and power as one serves.

Day 30 – Service

Out of the Backseat

"Always give yourselves fully to the work of the Lord, because you know that your labor in the Lord is not in vain." –1 Cor 15:58b (NIV)

A man was driving along on a rural road one summer day when he saw a car with a flat tire pulled over on the shoulder. Beside the car stood a young lady looking in dismay at what was left of the tire. The man decided to be a Good Samaritan, like the one in Luke 10:30-36, and pulled over to help. He became hot, and the sweat made the dirt cling to his clothes and skin.

The woman, who had been watching him, spoke up as he was finishing: "Be sure to let the jack down gently, because my husband is sleeping in the backseat of the car!" Cute story? Sure…but not when you apply it to the church! Sometimes we're a little too content to be napping when we ought to wake up, climb out of the backseat, and help change the tire!

That's certainly how Paul concludes 1 Corinthians 15. In this chapter he presents a systematic argument for the reality of the coming bodily resurrection. The certainty of our future resurrection from the dead— guaranteed by the past resurrection of Christ—leads to at least four sweeping principles that affect all of life: (1) truth is stronger than falsehood, (2) good is stronger than evil, (3) love is stronger than hatred, and (4) life is stronger than death.

Based upon these immutable truths, Paul concludes with the very timely exhortation of v. 58. In the first half of the verse, he says to be "firm" and "immovable," that is, to be well-grounded in biblical truths (like our future resurrection) and stable in our faith. But that doesn't mean we're to be stagnant or apathetic, for he quickly adds: "Always give yourselves fully to the work of the Lord." God wants us to voluntarily and continually be pouring all of ourselves into His service. And then comes the reason: "because you know that your labor in the Lord is not in vain" (v. 58b).

In other words, get and stay out of the backseat, because no effort in service to God is ever wasted! No resource spent, no time invested, no sacrifice made for Him is useless! Of all the things we could do in life—including "sleep away" the opportunities to serve—what else could we do that's *never* wasted?

For Discussion: Why do some "stay asleep in the backseat" rather than pitch in to help "change the tire" (the world)? Discuss how implications of the future resurrection (cf. 15:32) and key words in v. 58 address those reasons: "always," "give yourselves," "fully," "work of the Lord," "labor," "not in vain."

Day 31 – Service

From Squirting to Soaking

"Whatever you do, do your work heartily, as for the Lord rather than for men, knowing that from the Lord you will receive the reward of the inheritance. It is the Lord Christ whom you serve." –Col 3:23-24 (NAS)

Although they're valid and valuable (see yesterday), not every act of service should be "small." The Danish philosopher Soren Kierkegaard once wrote about a town where a fireman lived. Everyone liked the fireman because he was a nice guy who made it a habit to be gentle and kind, which was unusual for the rugged firemen of the day.
There was a fire one day, and the fireman charged to the scene with his fellow firemen and heavy equipment. As they came toward the fire, much to their surprise, they encountered between themselves and the flames about 200 townspeople. Each was aiming a water pistol at the raging fire, going "squirt, squirt, squirt."

The fireman asked, "What's going on here?" A spokesman for the group piped up, "Well, we all appreciate the wonderful work you're doing in our community, and each of us has come to contribute in some small way to your work." Squirt, squirt, squirt…they continued.

The fireman said, "I don't get it. You're all crazy!" The spokesman shot back, "Oh, we realize that we all could do more, but we just wanted to offer a token of our support." Everyone nodded. Squirt, squirt, squirt. "You don't know what you're doing!" shouted the fireman. "True, but you have to appreciate the fact that everyone is willing to offer whatever help they can," said the spokesman. Everyone said, "Amen!" and continued squirting. At that, the fireman told them all to get lost: "This is no picnic, this is a fire. And a fire doesn't require well-meaning people who come to make small contributions. A fire is a place where people come to give their lives!"

Ministry is serious business! It's so much so that the Lord wants us to put all of ourselves into whatever work we do. We should view each task as a labor of love for God rather than for people. That will radically affect the motive and quality of our work, because only He can give the heavenly reward that lasts forever (e.g., Matt 16:27; John 12:26; 1 Cor 3:7-15; Rev 22:12)!

For Discussion: Are you ever like the townspeople? Is there something you've been "squirting at" that you know you should be "dousing?"

Family Activity: Try to water flowers or clean dishes with squirt guns or spray bottles. Then do it with the hose or faucet. Discuss how this is like two ways to minister and how and why we should do the latter.

Day 32 – Service

Saving Starfish

"He who is faithful in a very little thing is faithful also in much."
–Luke 16:10 (NAS)

There was a little boy happily skipping along the beach one afternoon. Suddenly he came upon thousands of starfish that were stranded on the sand as the tide receded. They were all doomed, because they couldn't survive out of the water in the baking sun until the next high tide. When the boy realized this, he frantically started picking up starfish one by one and throwing them back in the water. He couldn't just stand by while God's creatures shriveled up and died.

A man walking along the beach saw the boy and hollered, "Son, what do you think you're doing? Don't you know there are thousands of starfish on this beach—and the beach goes on for miles? You're wasting your time. There's no way you can save all those starfish!" The little boy thought for a moment. Then he turned to the man, picked up a starfish, and said, "Yeah, I know. But I can save *this* one!" And he heaved that little creature as far as he could into the water.

One "excuse" that keeps us "napping in the backseat" (see last two days) instead of vigorously serving is the defeating thought that what we can offer is too small or petty to be worth much. To that, D. L. Moody said: "A good many are kept out of the service of Christ, deprived of the luxury of working for God, because they are trying to do some great thing. Let us be willing to do little things. And let us remember that nothing is small in which God is the source." Just ask one of those saved starfish! Likewise, A. T. Robertson wrote: "Whatever is done for God...must... be tested by three propositions: Is it work from God, as given us to do from Him; for God, as finding in Him its secret of power; and with God, as only a part of His work in which we engage as co-workers with Him?" No matter how "small" something is, it is "hardcore *ministry*" if it meets those criteria! And when we're faithful in using what God has given us to carry out the little things—even something like gathering firewood on a cold day (cf. Acts 28:1-3), He'll trust us with even more!

For Discussion: What is your attitude toward "small" acts of service?

Family Activity: Decide on a simple ministry project that you could do together as a family. You could start with something that's an act of love (John 13:34-35), hospitality (Rom 12:13), goodness (Gal 6:10), appreciation (Col 1:3), giving (2 Cor 9:12-13), or encouragement (1 Thess 5:11). Then do it!

MEET ME IN THE MORNING

Day 33 – Service

Glitzy Gifts and People Pleased

"My Father will honor the one who serves me." –John 12:26b (NIV)

The New York Post reported that producers of the 2002 Grammy ceremony showered each of the show's stars with a personalized gift basket worth at least $16,000! For example, Britney Spears got a pair of $1,900 diamond earrings, a Blackberry pager, an iPod MP3 player, a free two-night stay in the Ian Schrager hotel of her choice, and some Tic Tac mints. Janet Jackson and the guys of 'N Sync all received a one-year bi-coastal membership to Sports Club/L.A. (a $4,500 value) and a personalized bust of themselves. The other stars also got glitzy gift baskets.

Some years earlier, a famous pianist gave a concert in a renowned concert hall. When he finished, everyone gave him a rousing standing ovation. Well, almost everyone. There was an old man in the front row that didn't stand or cheer. The pianist began crying when he walked off the stage. His manager asked him what was wrong, to which he replied, "Didn't you see the man in the front row that wasn't standing or applauding?" The manager said, "Sure, I saw him. But he was the only one person in the whole place!" The pianist hung his head and said, "You don't understand. That man was the composer of the music I played tonight. He is the only one who counts. He's the only one who knows what the piece is supposed to sound like."

When some Christians serve, they hunger for the overflowing "gift baskets" of this world and the roaring cheers of the crowd.

DEEPENING YOUR DEVOTION TO GOD

That's how they measure their success and derive their satisfaction. Frankly, they're thinking way too *small*! If Grammy Award stars are honored so extravagantly for entertaining, can you imagine the reward for those who use their talents for eternal matters? And if the applause of the crowds is encouraging, how much more heartening is the applause of the One who *made* the crowds?

Scripture is clear: we should wholeheartedly seek to please *God*, covet *His* applause, and eagerly await *His* reward. Glitzy gifts and people pleased feel good for a moment. But they just don't compare with God saying to us: "Well done, good and faithful servant! You have been faithful with a few things; I will put you in charge of many things. Come and share your master's happiness!" (Matt 25:21, 23; cf. 3:17; John 5:30).

For Discussion: Talk about how these verses have or should affect your ministry actions and attitudes: Matt 6:1-6; 2 Cor 5:9-10; Gal 1:10; Col 3:24; 1 Thess 2:4-6a; Rev 22:12. (Time and interest permitting, continue with Matt 5:12; 16:27; 25:14-30; 1 Cor 3:7-15; 2 John 8.)

Day 34 – Service

Basin Theology

"[Jesus] poured water into a basin and began to wash his disciples' feet, drying them with the towel that was wrapped round him."
–John 13:5 (NIV)

A pastor of a church in Pittsburgh recently presented a message series about giving and serving. He shared a conversation with an active member of his church who approached him afterwards, saying: "When you get right down to it, it all comes down to basin theology." The pastor asked, "Basin theology? What's that?" The man replied, "Remember what Pilate did when he had the chance to acquit Jesus? He called for a basin and washed his hands of the whole thing [Matt 27:24]. But Jesus, the night before His death, called for a basin and proceeded to wash the feet of His disciples [read John 13:1-17]. It all comes down to basin theology: which one will you use?"

That man was right on! Every day two "basins" are presented for us to choose from. One is a basin that ignores the person and priorities of Jesus Christ. It is full of stuff but ultimately empty. Yet it is a fairly attractive basin to many, because it disregards the Lord's claims of rulership to our lives (e.g. 1 Cor 6:20; 7:23). It is also a dead-end and deadly basin (e.g., Jas 1:13-15).

Beside it sits a more modest and yet more honorable basin. It is one that beckons us to imitate Christ's stirring posture of servanthood, when He humbly washed His disciples' dusty feet—an unpleasant task reserved for the lowest servant of the house (John 13:1ff; cf. Phil 2:5ff). His "gentle and humble heart"

DEEPENING YOUR DEVOTION TO GOD

(Matt 11:29) prompted humble service to meet a practical need (clean feet!) as an example for the apostles and us to do the same (John 13:14-15; Rom 12:9-11). In God's economy, that includes leaders too (e.g., Mark 10:35-45)! If you ask 100 people what they'd do for a living if they could choose anything, you'll get about 100 different answers. Yet hardly ever will someone offer, "I want to be a servant."

Spiritually speaking, however, that is a "blessed" status (John 13:17). More importantly, it's the basin our Master chose (e.g., Matt 20:28; Mark 10:45; Luke 22:27; Phil 2:5ff). He's challenging you to choose the same one. Will you wash your hands in Pilate's basin, or wash others' feet in Jesus' basin?

For Discussion: What are some recent examples you've seen of a Christian "washing another's feet?" To whom and how can you humbly show practical love to a fellow Christian this week?

Family Activity: Who in your family needs his/her feet washed today? (Pause for giggles about who has the smelliest feet!) Seriously, who has a practical need that you could all humbly help meet?

Thanksgiving

Memory Verse:
*"Oh, give thanks to the LORD! Call upon His name;
make known His deeds among the peoples!"*
–Psalm 105:1 (NKJ)

Reading through the NT in 40 Days

- James .... Day 35
- 1 Peter .... Day 36
- 2 Peter – 1 John .... Day 37
- 2 John – Revelation 6 .... Day 38
- Revelation 7-14 .... Day 39
- Revelation 15-22 .... Day 40

**"Gratitude is the least remembered of all virtues and the acid test of your character."
-Elmer Towns**

MEET ME IN THE MORNING

Day 35 – Thanksgiving

Thank You, Thank You, Thank You

"Thanks be to God for His indescribable gift!"–2 Corinthians 9:15 (NKJ)

Imagine that you're on the Florida coast. The sun is setting like a gigantic orange ball as the water laps at the shore. The gentle breeze makes for a cool evening on the isolated stretch of beach. You look up and see an old man hobbling down the beach with a bucket. He walks to the old pier that stretches out in the water and looks up into the sky. A mass of dancing dots draws closer. The sea gulls are coming! The man takes handfuls of shrimp out of his bucket and throws them on the dock. The sea gulls land all around him—some even perch on his shoulders, others on his hat. His feathered friends linger long after the shrimp are gone.

What's going on here? Why does this man feed the sea gulls week after week? The man in that scene was Eddie Rickenbacher, a famous WWII pilot. His plane, *The Flying Fortress*, went down in 1942 and nobody thought he'd be rescued. Perhaps you've heard how he and his eight passengers escaped death by climbing into two rafts for thirty days. They fought extreme thirst, heat, even sharks as long as nine feet. But what nearly killed them first was starvation. Their scant rations were totally gone within eight days.

Rickenbacher wrote that even on those rafts they would have an afternoon prayer and devotional time every day. After this time one day, Rickenbacher leaned back and put his hat over his eyes and tried to get some sleep. Within a few moments he felt something on his head. He knew in an instant it was a sea gull. How it got there—hundreds of miles out to sea—he didn't know. But he was certain that if he didn't get that sea gull he would die. Soon the others noticed the bird. No one spoke, no one moved. Rickenbacher quickly grabbed the sea gull. They ate the flesh of that bird with much thanksgiving. They used its intestines for fish bait and managed to survive.

Rickenbacher never forgot that visitor, that sacrificial guest from a far away place. Every week he went out on the pier with a full bucket of shrimp and said thank you, thank you, thank you!

For Discussion: In your own words, together relate this story to the sacrifice of Jesus for us. Then, talk about how Rickenbacher's grateful response should be like ours. How can and will you say "thank you,' thank you, thank you" to God?!

MEET ME IN THE MORNING

Day 36 – Thanksgiving

Too Good to Keep to Ourselves

"Oh, give thanks to the LORD! Call upon His name; make known His deeds among the peoples!" –Psalm 105:1 (NKJ)

Can you remember hearing or experiencing something *so* good that you just couldn't stop thinking and talking about it? Peter and John can relate! In Acts 3 they healed a crippled beggar, who "jumped to his feet and began to walk [and] went with them into temple courts, walking and jumping, and praising God" (v. 8). As you can imagine, all those who were accustomed to seeing this man begging every day at the temple gate "were filled with wonder and amazement at what had happened to him…and came running to them" (vv. 10-11; read 3:1-4:31).

As expected, the religious rulers "were greatly disturbed because the apostles were teaching the people and proclaiming…Jesus" (4:2). So, "they seized Peter and John…[and] put them in jail" (v. 3). The next day they were "called to account" for the miracle done in Jesus' power (v. 9). Although their very lives were threatened, they continued to courageously proclaim Christ. And since the rulers "could see the man who had been healed standing there with them…[and] everybody living in Jerusalem [knew] they [had] done an outstanding miracle" (vv. 14, 16), all they could do was order "them not to speak or teach at all in the name of Jesus" (v. 18).

What would you say with *your* life on the line? Their response is heartening: "We cannot help speaking about what we have seen and heard" (v. 20). In other words, their grateful amazement at Jesus and His power was just *too good* to keep to themselves!

DEEPENING YOUR DEVOTION TO GOD

In today's verse and many others, a connection is made between giving thanks to God and letting others know about it. Some have gone as far as to say that unexpressed gratitude is worthless! Not only are we to "give...thanks in the great assembly" of other believers (Ps 35:18), but even among "the nations"—people who may not share our gratitude or revere our God (Ps 105:1). What do we proclaim? As in Acts 4, the psalmist suggests you include "the wonders he has done, his miracles, and the judgments he pronounced" (v. 5). Who God is and what He's done is just too good to keep to ourselves!

To Do and Discuss: Brainstorm several of God's wonders, miracles, and judgments in history and your life that you are (or should be!) thankful for. Then pick a person (Christian or not) with whom you could share something you're grateful to God for this week. Finally, do it!

Day 37 – Thanksgiving

A Recipe for Giving Thanks

"How can we thank God enough for you in return for all the joy we have in the presence of our God because of you?" –1 Thess 3:9 (NIV)

Nobody could accuse me of being a chef, but I know that the right ingredients and recipe are critical to a dish's success. Heloise wrote in her "hints" column that the best way to cook a moist turkey is to "put a cup of water in the cavity of the turkey, cover with tin foil and bake." A reader wrote back to complain: "The turkey came out fine, but the plastic cup in the turkey melted!" What a reminder that directions must be specific!

Fortunately, the Bible gives us some specifics for a "recipe of thankfulness" to others. (By the way, this also applies to thanking God!) Glance at Nehemiah 3. It is a chapter you might easily skip over. It seems rather long and a bit monotonous. Yet the repetitive and comprehensive nature shows four lessons for giving thanks to others.

Be Specific – Nehemiah (a) puts in writing (b) each name and (c) their specific contribution to the rebuilding of the Jerusalem city walls. If you want just one example, read v. 15. Now *that's* specific gratitude! Paul also frequently thanks God for those he's writing to. And when he does, he always mentions *why* (e.g., Rom 1:8; Phil 1:3-5; Col 1:3-12; 1 Thess 1:2-3; 2 Thess 1:3; Phile 4-5).

Be Singular – A "group thanks" can be meaningful. But singling out individuals—as Nehemiah and Paul (e.g., Rom. 16) did—shows them even more gratitude. Which would you rather have?

DEEPENING YOUR DEVOTION TO GOD

Be Sensitive – Nehemiah notes that "the people worked with all their heart" (4:6). The best words of thanks recognize not only the action but also the heart attitude behind the action. Jesus showed this when he noticed a child's humility, a widow who gave her last two mites, and a woman who poured perfume on His feet.

Be Searching – Nehemiah's sensitivity led him to be searching. He searched out and noticed each person and their unique contribution. That's why the chapter is so long! Most of us have already planned our Thanksgiving menu. But have we planned who we'll express thanks to and how? Let's take some time to fill in the ingredients for this "thanksgiving recipe."

To Discuss and Do: Have everyone share at least one other person they're thankful for and why. Then make a plan to express your gratitude to those people by the end of this week. Do it "Nehemiah style!"

Day 38 – Thanksgiving

Thankful Praise to Our Good God

"Praise the LORD! Oh give thanks to the LORD, for He is good; For His lovingkindness is everlasting."–Psalm 106:1 (NAS)

For all our moral stumbling, many people know excellence when they see it and are overwhelmed by the magnetism of goodness. Goodness attracts.

It is proclaimed so that the circle of adulation can widen. That's why we have film critics who laud good movies and restaurant critics who highlight where to get a fine meal. When an athlete shows excellence, sports fans find it irresistible. Excellence is magnetic and powerful!

We like good things. Perhaps that's why so very few people have ever scratched their heads over the presence of goodness. We routinely hear, "Why is there evil in the world? Why do bad things happen?" But when was the last time you heard someone cry out, "How can you explain the presence of excellence? Why do *good* things happen to people?"

Theologians and philosophers wrestle with the so-called "problem of evil," but the "problem of goodness" does not exist. Why? It's because "The LORD is good to all, and His tender mercies are over all His works. ... The eyes of all look expectantly to you, and you give them their food in due season. You open your hand and satisfy the desire of every living thing" (Ps 145:9, 15-16; cf. Jas 1:17). That is partly why it's such a callous insult not to thankfully acknowledge God (Rom 1:18-32), especially since He remains "kind to the unthankful and evil" (Luke 6:35) —not to mention to His children!

There are at least 140 biblical references to giving thanks to God, thirty five in the Psalms alone. Added together, some form of "thanks" and "praise" are mentioned 461 times, often in the same breath (e.g., 1 Chron 23:30; 29:13; Ps 30:4; 100:4). How often are those words—or at least those sentiments—in *our* breaths?

Although we could look at many examples, Daniel was a great man of prayer and praise. His prayer shows three specific ways "to give thanks and praise" to God (Dan 2:23); namely, to thankfully praise God for (1) His timeless character, (2) His present work in your life, and (3) His past actions in history (see vv. 19-23). That alone should keep you busy thankfully praising for a lifetime...and eternity (cf. Rev 4:8-5:14)!

For Discussion: Brainstorm and journal several responses to the three aspects of thankful praise. Then pray a prayer incorporating them.

Family Activity: Turn to Psalm 136. Have an adult read the first half of each verse, while the rest of the family echoes the refrain in the second half. Give it some "grateful gusto!"

Day 39 – Thanksgiving

An Attitude of Gratitude

"…always giving thanks to God the Father for everything, in the name of our Lord Jesus Christ." –Ephesians 5:20 (NIV)

"I like to play with the stars," a little girl told her pastor one day when he visited. She was confined to a bed because of a severe spinal deformity. At her request, her bed had been thoughtfully positioned so that she could see the sky out of her window. "I wake up a lot at night and can't get back to sleep," she said. "That's when I play with the stars." Curious about what she meant, her pastor asked, "How do you play with the stars?" The child answered, "I pick out one and say, 'That's Mommy.'

I see another one and say, 'That's Daddy.' And I just keep on naming the stars after people and things I'm thankful for—my brothers and sisters, my doctor, my friends, my dog." She continued on and on until at last she exclaimed, "But there just aren't enough stars to go around!" Now *that's* an attitude of gratitude!

Do you ever feel that way when you think about the many blessings God has showered on you? We could never name all of our physical, temporal, spiritual, and eternal blessings. But I'm convinced that God wants us to try sometimes! Thanksgiving begins with a good memory, which is why so many Thanksgiving Psalms extol God's past actions (see Lam 3:21-23).

In case you're afraid you'll run out of things to say, answer Paul's question to the Corinthians, "What do you have that you did not receive?" (1 Cor 4:7b). The correct response? Nothing! On top of honoring the Source of those gifts, I learned how therapeutic an attitude of gratitude is for the thanker. During an especially difficult period in my teens, I was challenged to write a daily gratitude list. Nothing fancy; just to jot down ten things I was thankful for each morning. Shortly, I was up to twenty or more. Some things were repeated, others were unique. Over time, I filled an entire notebook. (I just re-read it for the first time in years. I'm bursting with gratitude!) My perspective changed and my world lightened as I trained myself to focus on God's good grace.

I just made a new entry in that old notebook…and I agree: "there just aren't enough stars to go around!"

To Discuss and Do: Keep Thanksgiving alive long after the turkey leftovers are gone! Let me challenge you to join my family in making a daily gratitude list between now and Christmas. Then review it together at Christmas when you celebrate the greatest gift—the birth of Jesus Christ! (For younger kids, consider making "God's gift to me" stickers. Let them place a few on different things each day.) Why not grab a notepad and start that list today?

Day 40 – Thanksgiving

Taking the Time To Say Thanks

"One of them, when he saw he was healed, came back, praising God in a loud voice. He threw himself at Jesus' feet and thanked him."

–Luke 17:15-16a (read vv. 11-19) (NIV)

In those days, lepers were quarantined in colonies because their disease was so awful and contagious. That's why the ten lepers "stood at a distance" and "called out in a loud voice" for Jesus to have pity on them (vv. 12-13). Upon hearing them, Jesus prescribed for them to follow the Law of Moses and go see the priests, who would determine their fitness to rejoin normal society.

Amazingly, their miraculous healing from their horrible condition occurred as the men obeyed in faith (v. 14, 19). However, only "one of them, when he saw he was healed, came back, praising God in a loud voice. He threw himself at Jesus' feet and thanked him" (vv. 15-16a). What's even more striking is that this man "was a Samaritan" (v. 16b; cf. v. 18). Samaritans and Jews had long been at spiritual odds, and yet this man bowed gratefully to Jesus, a Jew. His response to Jesus' good gift was the only right one (v. 19)!

The failure of the other nine to do the same (vv. 17-18) is a powerful depiction of the ugliness of ingratitude. Rather than thinking of thankfulness as a nice little virtue among many, God wants us to know that ingratitude is actually the behavior of those outside of Christ and an invitation to His wrath

(Rom 1:18-21). Thanklessness is even a sign of the "terrible times in the last days" (2 Tim 3:1-2)! Christians, on the other hand, are to "give thanks in all circumstances, for this is God's will for you in Christ Jesus" (1 Thess 5:18; cf. Eph 5:20).

God wants us to be like "the one" who returned. However, we can sometimes see ourselves among those nine lepers, can't we? We're anxious to receive but careless about giving thanks in return. I can imagine those nine lepers each having a reason for not returning: "I was waiting to see if the cure was real. I wanted to see if it would last. I thought I'd see Jesus later. I must not have really had leprosy to begin with. I would have gotten well anyway. The priests were the ones who really healed me. Any rabbi could have done it. I was already getting better. I was too embarrassed to return. I just followed the crowd. I forgot." What a contrast between that and the one who took time to promptly give sincere thanks to the Source of his blessing. Will you be like "the one"?

To Discuss and Do: What does it feel like when people "forget" to say thanks for something special you've done for them? Is there something you've "forgotten" to thank God for? Today is the perfect day to do it!

Appendix A: Suggestions for Family Devotions

Family devotions often seem more like chaos than church! Keep in mind that your goal isn't perfection. If your home is as active as mine, your aim should probably be more like "holy confusion with a purpose"— namely, to understand and apply something of the biblical thoughts for that day.

Here are a few suggestions that can help you accomplish that.

1. Choose a consistent time and place. Whether it's at the breakfast table or in a child's room before bedtime, having devotions at the same time and place each day is the best way to be consistent. It'll become a habit after just a couple weeks of practice. So choose the best time and place for *your* family…and stick to it!

2. Don't worry if you miss a day. It will probably happen; maybe more than once. Although you *can* complete forty consecutive devotions, you may want to try to double-up if you get behind. By intention, the devotions typically don't build upon each other. Plus, this booklet is yours to keep…and I doubt God would mind if you have to go a little past the forty days to finish!

3. Parent(s) take the lead! This is a great time to exercise spiritual leadership. God and your children are counting on you to "bring them up in the training and instruction of the Lord" (Eph 6:4)!

4. Involve the whole family. Leadership doesn't mean domination! Although parents should take the initiative, work to include the whole family in every way possible. Take turns praying, reading the devotions, and looking up verses. Encourage everyone to share in the discussions and activities. The greater the participation, the greater the ownership…and the growth!

5. Modifications are allowed! You know your family far better than I, so don't be bashful about tweaking this booklet. We'll all want and need to explain, adjust, and expand the devotions according to the age, interests, abilities, maturity, and number of our family members. You may want to spend a few minutes before each family time considering how you can best communicate that day's lesson. Along that line, be sure to bring the lesson to bear on your family's "real life," which is what God desires.

6. Pray before and/or after each devotion. The combination of the Word and prayer will produce far more results than we could even begin to manufacture in our own strength! You may also want to sing a hymn or praise song, write a poem, do a craft, draw a picture, make up a story, act out a skit, or do some other creative reinforcement in preparation for or response to some devotions.

7. Finally, be yourselves! It's perfectly fine to laugh and have some fun. The kids will soak up lots more truth in that atmosphere, and it will let some pressure off you.

Take these tips to heart…and let me know sometime how it's going with your family!

"Love the LORD your God with all your heart and with all your soul and with all your strength. These commandments that I give you today are to be upon your hearts. Impress them on your children. Talk about them when you sit at home and when you walk along the road, when you lie down and when you get up. Tie them as symbols on your hands and bind them on your foreheads. Write them on the door-frames of your houses and on your gates."–Deuteronomy 6:5-9

Appendix B: Forty Day New Testament Reading Plan

"[The Scriptures] shall be his constant companion. He must read from it everyday of his life so that he will learn to respect the Lord his God by obeying all of His commands."
–Deut 17:19 (LB)

"Your Word is a lamp to my feet and a light for my path."
–Ps 119:105 (NIV)

"Let the Words of Christ, in all their richness, live in your hearts and make you wise. Use his words to teach and counsel each other."–Col 3:16a (NLT)

"All Scripture is God-breathed and is useful for teaching, rebuking, correcting and training in righteousness, so that the man of God may be thoroughly equipped for every good work."
–2 Tim 3:16-17 (NIV)

"He blesses all who listen to [this book] and obey what it says."
–Rev 1:3b (NLT)

- Matthew 1-5 .... (Mon-Day 1)
- Matthew 6-11 .... (Tues-Day 2)
- Matthew 12-17 .... (Wed-Day 3)
- Matthew 18-23 .... (Thurs-Day 4)
- Matthew 24-28 .... (Fri-Day 5)
- Mark 1-8 .... (Sat-Day 6)
- Mark 9-16 .... (Sun-Day 7)
- Luke 1-6 .... (Mon-Day 8)
- Luke 7-12 .... (Tues-Day 9)
- Luke 13-18 .... (Wed-Day 10)

MEET ME IN THE MORNING

- Luke 19-24 .... (Thurs-Day 11)
- John 1-5 .... (Fri-Day 12)
- John 6-10 .... (Sat-Day 13)
- John 11-16 .... (Sun-Day 14)
- John 17-22 .... (Mon-Day 15)
- Acts 1-5 .... (Tues-Day 16)
- Acts 6-11 .... (Wed-Day 17)
- Acts 12-17 .... (Thurs-Day 18)
- Acts 18-23 .... (Fri-Day 19)
- Acts 24-28 .... (Sat-Day 20)
- Romans 1-8 .... (Sun-Day 21)
- Romans 9-16 .... (Mon-Day 22)
- 1 Corinthians 1-8 .... (Tues-Day 23)
- 1 Corinthians 9-16 .... (Wed-Day 24)
- 2 Corinthians 1-6 .... (Thurs-Day 25)
- 2 Corinthians 7-13 .... (Fri-Day 26)
- Galatians .... (Sat-Day 27)
- Ephesians .... (Sun-Day 28)
- Philippians – Col .... (Mon-Day 29)
- 1 – 2 Thess .... (Tues-Day 30)
- 1 Timothy .... (Wed-Day 31)
- 2 Tim – Phile .... (Thurs-Day 32)
- Hebrews 1-6 .... (Fri-Day 33)
- Hebrews 7-13 .... (Sat-Day 34)
- James .... (Sun-Day 35)
- 1 Peter............................ (Mon-Day 36)
- 2 Peter – 1 John .... (Tues-Day 37)
- 2 John – Rev 6 .... (Wed-Day 38)
- Revelation 7-14 .... (Thurs-Day 39)
- Revelation 15-22 .... (Fri-Day 40)

Appendix D: Six Key Memory Verses

Following the kickoff of the Forty Days, each of the following memory verses corresponds to the main theme of the six weeks. Let's put the memory tips into action (Appendix C) by etching these words on our souls during the days listed:

Week One

COMMITMENT
2 Chronicles 16:9a - "The eyes of the LORD search the whole earth in order to strengthen those whose hearts are fully committed to him." (NLT)

Week Two

FAITH
Hebrews 11:1 - "Now faith is being sure of what we hope for and certain of what we do not see." (NIV)

Week Three

SACRIFICE
2 Corinthians 8:7 - "But just as you excel in everything - in faith, in speech, in knowledge, in complete earnestness and in your love for us - see that you also excel in this grace of giving." (NIV)

Week Four

PURPOSE
Philippians 2:13 - "For it is God who works in you to will and to act according to his good purpose." (NIV)

Week Five

SERVICE
1 Corinthians 15:58b - "Always give yourselves fully to the work of the Lord, because you know that your labor in the Lord is not in vain." (NIV)

Week Six

THANKSGIVING
Psalms 105:1 - "Oh, give thanks to the LORD! Call upon His name; make known His deeds among the peoples!" (NKJ)

Appendix C: Tips for Bible Memorization

One of the most effective ways to drive deeply into our lives the principles we are learning during this campaign is to memorize key verses that correspond to each theme. For some, Bible memorization is a new concept or one that has been difficult in the past. Others in our church have locked in their hearts the treasure of 100's of verses, serving as both an example and encouragement to the rest of us. Whatever your history has been with memorization, I want to urge you to stretch yourself by committing these six powerful verses to memory. You can do it!

1. For perspective and motivation, familiarize yourself with how incredibly important Bible memory actually is. You can start by investigating Deut 6:6-9; 11:18-21; Josh 1:7-8; Job 22:22; Ps 1:2-3; 37:30-31; 40:8; 119:11; Prov 7:2-3; Jer 9:24; Matt 4:4; John 15:7; Phil 4:19; Col 3:16; and Heb 4:12.

2. Seek to understand the author's meaning and the personal application(s) of the verse.

3. Aim to memorize the verse word-perfect.

4. Work with a partner or group for accountability, help, enjoyment, and celebration over success.

5. Say the reference before and after the verse each time you recite it.

6. Read the verse out loud—again and again.

7. Write the verse down multiple times. Keep it in your possession, like on a flash card in your pocket, for regular review.

8. Break the verse into natural units or phrases to make the memory more manageable.

9. When you say it, emphasize key words—the anchors of the verse.

10. Display the verse everywhere you spend time—your car's dash, your bathroom mirror, your computer monitor, the refrigerator, etc.

11. Review, review, review! How do we cement God's Word in our minds? By constant review!

12. Have fun and be creative with the memory!

Appendix D: Personal Notes / Prayer Journal On Faith

Appendix E: Personal Notes / Prayer Journal On Commitment

Appendix F: Personal Notes / Prayer Journal On Purpose

Appendix G: Personal Notes / Prayer Journal On Sacrifice

Appendix H: Personal Notes / Prayer Journal On Service

Appendix I: Personal Notes / Prayer Journal On Thanksgiving